CW00890325

Keynes

Keynes

Robert Cord

HAUS PUBLISHING · LONDON

First published in Great Britain in 2007 by
Haus Publishing Limited
26 Cadogan Court
Draycott Avenue
London SW3 3BX
www.hauspublishing.co.uk

Copyright © Robert Cord 2007

The moral right of the author has been asserted

A CIP catalogue record for this book is available from the British Library

ISBN 978-1-905791-00-2

Typeset in Garamond 3 by MacGuru Ltd
info@macguru.org.uk

Printed in Dubai by Oriental Press

Front cover: Getty Images

Contents

To my mother, with love

Acknowledgements

I would like to thank Elizabeth Ennion at the King's College Archives for her help in tracking down some of the material quoted in this book. I also owe a debt of gratitude to Geoff Harcourt at Cambridge, a unique source of advice, guidance and wisdom on everything Keynes.

Origins and Education 1883–1905

John Maynard Keynes was born at 6 Harvey Road in Cambridge on 5 June 1883. Maynard, as he was to become known – only his mother called him John – was the eldest of three children of John Neville Keynes and Florence Ada Keynes. The Keynes's middle child, Margaret, was born 14 months after Maynard. She would marry the Noble Prize-winning physiologist A V Hill. The youngest child, Geoffrey, entered the world in March 1887. He was to make his name as one of England's foremost surgeons, and by marrying Charles Darwin's granddaughter Margaret in 1917 was to join together two of England's most distinguished intellectual families. The Keynes's were clearly high achievers, a quality that was to find its most complete realisation in the life and career of Maynard, not only as a world-renowned economist but also as a civil servant, businessman, supporter of the arts, and perhaps the most distinguished product of Cambridge of his era.

Maynard's immediate ancestry was certainly favourable. His father John Neville Keynes was born in August 1852, the only son of John Keynes and Anna Maynard Neville. John Keynes had put the family finances on a firmer footing through his success as a florist in Salisbury. Neville showed early academic promise which led to enrolment first at London University and then in 1872 at Pembroke College, Cambridge, on a scholarship to read mathematics. He soon came to dislike the tough regime of Cambridge's mathematical teaching, however, and switched to the moral sciences, a subject that allowed a student to study not only moral philosophy but also political economy, the forerunner of economics. Neville took to it like a duck to water, achieving first place and the title of Senior Moralist in the examinations of 1875. Such an impressive performance was usually the sign of great things to come and Neville did indeed produce some important works, notably *Studies and Exercises in Formal Logic* (1884) and *The Scope and Method of Political Economy* which appeared in 1890 and became the 'standard English treatise on the subject'.[1] In later years, he became a highly efficient administrator in his role as the Registrary (administrative head) at Cambridge, a position he held for 15 years. Unfortunately, a certain lack of ambition, a desire to stay out of the limelight and a fear of stress meant that he never completely fulfilled his true potential.

Florence Keynes (née Brown) was born in March 1861. Her temperament was wholly different from her husband's. She possessed a good intellect, reflected in her admission as one of the earliest students at the recently founded all-female Newnham Hall (now Newnham College) in Cambridge, a product of the many reforms implemented at the University during the 19th century. As the daughter of John Brown, a well-known Congregationalist minister from the north of England, Florence had inherited a concern for the welfare of others, which became the focus of her activities after marrying Neville. This was to manifest itself in the many charities she became involved in, such as the Papworth Village Settlement which helped tuberculosis sufferers. With her public profile already high, Florence would go on to become mayoress of Cambridge. Thus while Maynard may have inherited his father's strong intellectual turn of mind and his abilities as an administrator, his mother gave him an acute appreciation and sympathy for the plight of others, a characteristic which was to so often show itself during his life. Sadly, Maynard never inherited his parents' longevity: both lived into their nineties, long enough to see their eminent son pass away in his early sixties.

The network of people in Neville and Florence's circle in Cambridge was extensive and included some of the most illustrious thinkers of the time. As a youngster growing up in the town, it was inevitable that Maynard would have been impressed and influenced by such figures. With important people regularly popping in for tea and conversation, Maynard must have felt the weight of expectation on his shoulders. Amongst the regular visitors to the Keynes household were the philosophers Henry Sidgwick and W E Johnson, and the economist Herbert Foxwell. For Neville, perhaps his most interesting, albeit troubling, relationship was with his former tutor, Alfred Marshall, the greatest economist of the late 19th and early 20th centuries, founder of the Cambridge School of Economics, and later also the teacher of the undergraduate Maynard. Although Marshall came from a relatively humble background, his early brilliance as a mathematician secured him a place at Cambridge, where in 1865 he was placed Second Wrangler, i.e. second amongst those achieving a First Class degree in the Mathematics Tripos (or exams). The Senior Wrangler for that year was John William Strutt, who was later to become the eminent scientist Lord Rayleigh.

Although Marshall was to enjoy a relatively good relationship with Maynard, his ties with Neville and Florence were less solid. In all the Keynes's many years of entertaining at Harvey Road, Marshall was never once on the guest list, his visits being for official purposes only. Not deterred, Marshall thought very highly of Neville, regarding him as 'one of the best two or three students he had ever had'.[2] Neville did not return the compliment. He was irritated by Marshall's attempts to persuade him to move to Oxford, no doubt suspecting that Marshall hoped that, once there, Neville would spread the Marshallian gospel. Neville was also put off by Marshall's shenanigans when it came to running the economics department at Cambridge, describing Marshall as 'a dreadful bore', 'exceedingly irrelevant' and 'the most exasperating talker I know'.[3] Harsh words indeed!

Despite these apparent personality failings, Marshall was a man on a mission. To begin with, he produced some of the most influential theoretical work in economics ever written. His *magnum opus* was *The Principles of Economics*, published in 1890. The *Principles* was to form an important element in the 'neoclassical' revolution in economic thinking, started in the 1870s, and which to this day continues to be a crucial part of every economist's training. Marshall also fought a long and eventually successful battle to get economics established as a stand-alone degree at Cambridge, a development which was to be crucial in the University's efforts to become one of the world's leading centres in the discipline. Indeed, without Marshall's exertions, it is doubtful that Cambridge could have produced such a revolutionary figure as Maynard Keynes.

Maynard's schooling began in 1889 when he was sent to the Perse School Kindergarten in Cambridge, his formal learning being supplemented by lessons at home from Neville, a recurring feature of his education right up to his graduation from Cambridge and beyond. This was followed in early 1892 by enrolment at St Faith's Preparatory School, also in Cambridge. Having been removed to Bedford for the autumn of 1893 due to his parents' concern that excessive schoolwork might be affecting his health, Maynard began to show considerable academic promise, especially in mathematics. After coming first in a maths examination in July 1894, the reports of Maynard's work by his teachers refer to his 'brilliance' such that by 1896 he is described as being 'head and shoulders above all the other boys in the school'.[4] This was also meant literally, as Maynard was already tall for his age, albeit somewhat lanky. He had a lasting fixation about his physical appearance, as well as an obsession with the appearance of people's hands, believing that they said a lot about a person's character. The first recorded reference to this fascination was in April 1899 when Maynard wrote to his father that he had had a conversation

Keynes's parents, John Neville Keynes and Florence Keynes, in 1944

with Sir George Darwin, son of Charles, and thought that *His hands certainly looked as if he might be descended from an ape.*[5] Always one for fairness, Maynard regarded his own looks as rather ugly, although others thought his face was interesting and sensitive, centred on his large dark blue eyes which were 'very beautiful – steady, direct and full of kindness and wisdom'.[6]

Given his academic gifts, the thoughts of Maynard's parents

and teachers quickly turned to the possibility of his obtaining a scholarship to Eton, England's most prestigious school. The entrance examination took place in July 1897 and lasted for a full three days. Maynard had been well drilled in what to expect and how to approach the exams by both his father and various teachers. His exam preparation would often start at 7 a.m., going somewhat against Maynard's natural propensity to sleep in. Once his son had sat the exams but before publication of the results, Neville, according to form, worried incessantly about whether Maynard had done well enough to secure a place. He needn't have worried: Maynard's efforts had secured him tenth place out of the 20 boys elected that year. Dillwyn Knox headed the list and it was Knox who was to become one of Maynard's earliest friends – and later probably his first lover – when Keynes started at Eton in September 1897.

Eton is a famous English public school for boys founded by King Henry VI in 1440. It has produced countless politicians and other notable public figures. Keynes attended the school from 1897 to 1902. Later, in 1940, he was made a Fellow of Eton, the cue for his becoming extensively involved in putting the school's finances on to a more sensible footing.

At his schools in Cambridge, Maynard had been comfortably ahead of the other boys. Eton now gave him the opportunity to test his intelligence against some of the country's elite. The social hierarchy amongst the boys was decided by a division between the so-called 'Oppidans' and 'Collegers', the former generally being from aristocratic backgrounds and thus fee-paying, whilst the latter, including Maynard, were at the school purely on merit. Despite his poor health, Maynard was a full participant in the social, athletic and intellectual activities provided by the school. Socially, his first achievement was to be placed at the head of a list for election to Chamber Pop, one of Eton's debating societies. This was followed in 1901 with the even higher accolade of being elected to the Eton Society, more popularly known as just Pop,

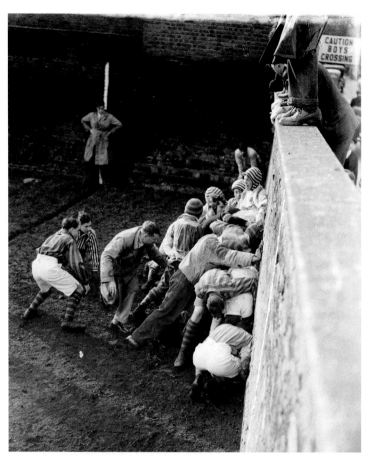

The Eton Wall Game, which Keynes found *glorious*

membership of which was preserved only for those with some social standing in the school.

He also quickly gathered around him a close-knit group of friends. As well as Knox, there was Robert Dundas, later a distinguished Greek historian at Oxford, and Bernard Swithinbank, who forged a career in the military. Maynard's attempts to keep this band of brothers in close contact with each other after they had left Eton – made easier in the case of Knox as both he and Keynes were at Cambridge together – was an early sign of the high regard he held for his friends.

On the sporting side, although not a natural athlete, Maynard displayed a keen interest. His enthusiasm for competitive physical activity was probably first ignited when his father introduced him to golf and he was to play a round with Sidgwick shortly before the philosopher's death. Maynard's obsessive keeping of his golf scores again highlighted his interest in numbers. Whilst at Eton his main sporting interests seem to have been rowing and cricket. He also participated in the infamous and unfathomable Eton Wall Game which he found *glorious* but which failed to impress his parents given the heavy physical exertion it demanded.

Of course, the main reason why Keynes was at Eton was because of his mind. Needless to say, his brilliance was undimmed by his new, more challenging surroundings. He won numerous prizes, totalling over 60 in his time at the school, with the focus not surprisingly being on mathematics. Indeed, the school only really taught two subjects to an advanced level, namely mathematics and classics. Maynard developed a love of poetry, backed up by what was to become an impressive book collection. It was Samuel Lubbock, Keynes's tutor at Eton, who was responsible for arousing these other interests. Lubbock had just returned to Eton after graduating with a First Class degree in Classics from King's College, Cambridge, and was handpicked by Neville as the man who could give his son the best education possible. At the same time, Neville left nothing to chance, acting as more or less a second tutor to Maynard during his years at Eton. Maynard didn't seem to mind the arrangement, writing home every few days to tell his father what he had been up to.

Despite poetry and other distractions, mathematics remained the focus of Maynard's intellectual endeavours. Thus it was no surprise that he sat and won the school's top mathematics prize, the Tomline, in June 1901. His work rate was becoming more intense such that by the time he sat for the Cambridge Higher Certificate in July of the same year he was regularly working for more than 10 hours a day. After securing first place in the certificate which ensured that a contribution would be made to his future university fees, Maynard had to choose where he would spend his undergraduate years. Having decided that he did not want to go Oxford *at any price*, it was to be either King's or Trinity College at Cambridge. As he was going to read mathematics, Trinity was perhaps the natural choice, given its outstanding tradition in the subject. For his part, Maynard had already set his sights on King's, perhaps reflecting Lubbock's influence and the fact that King's was the sister foundation of Eton which meant it awarded a handful of scholarships to boys from the school. Maynard decided to sit both the mathematics and classics examinations for King's, although it was more usual for only one paper to be offered. Again, he sailed through, his good performance in the classics paper helping to secure a scholarship. Although he was off to Cambridge, Eton would hold a special place in Keynes's heart for the rest of his life. On leaving it in the summer of 1902, he wrote that *I have just reached a very melancholy stage. Last night I received a vote of thanks in College Pop, which I think I desired perhaps more than anything else that remains to be got here. Eton has been much kinder to me than I deserve ...*[7]

Keynes's long association with King's College began in October 1902. Life at Cambridge was to play an important part in shaping the rest of his life: 'At Cambridge Maynard experienced a philosophic, aesthetic, and emotional awakening which shifted his values. He never lost his inherited sense of public duty, which his Eton education had reinforced. But from his undergraduate years onwards he was to balance this against the claims of leading a civilised life and of personal happiness, which sprang from the

King's College Chapel, Cambridge

emotional and philosophic atmosphere of his Cambridge world, and to which one part of him strongly responded. In this shift of values King's College played an important part.'[8]

King's had been founded in 1441 by King Henry VI, with its world-famous chapel being completed in the 16th century. It had a somewhat sleepy existence for a few hundred years but this all changed in the middle of the 19th century as the University authorities came under pressure to make the College more academically rigorous. With the renowned Trinity College just a stone's throw away, the powers that be at King's took it upon themselves to create an institution worthy of comparison. Reforms took place relatively quickly by Cambridge standards and by the time Keynes started his first undergraduate year, King's had become one of the most academically prestigious colleges at Cambridge. It also had its fair share of characters, notably Oscar Browning, a fellow in history, who was widely regarded as one of the most eccentric men in Cambridge, and Goldsworthy Lowes Dickinson, a young history don. Both of these Kingsmen encapsulated the spirit and practice of homosexuality which was common at King's at the time.

In his first year, Keynes moved into accommodation located on what was then known as King's Lane, one of the quieter parts of Cambridge. Never one to let his surroundings get him down, Keynes was quick to make friends with other Lane residents. Indeed, it was on the Lane that he met Robin Furness, who turned out to be perhaps his closest friend at King's. Also on the Lane was C R Fay, who was invited to tea by Keynes on their very first day as undergraduates, and J T Sheppard who would one day become Provost of King's. Keynes's ability to make friends easily was facilitated by his natural charm and also by the network he established as a result of his membership of many of the University's clubs and debating societies. Thus we see him making his debut at the Cambridge Union in late 1902, claiming it to be the *bravest thing I ever did* (of course, presidency of the Union soon followed); joining the Walpole Society, the best-known undergraduate society at Cambridge, and the Liberal Club; and being recruited to the Decemviri, a club for a select group of just 10 undergraduates from Trinity and King's.

However, it was Keynes's membership of the Cambridge Conversazione Society, or the 'Apostles', as it was better known, that was to have the greatest impact on him. The Apostles was founded by the Cambridge student and future Bishop of Gibraltar, George Tomlinson, in 1820, its name deriving from the fact that its original membership numbered 12. It quickly established itself as being prestigious. Previous members or 'angels' had included Alfred Lord Tennyson, James Clerk Maxwell and E M Forster; in later years the spies Guy Burgess and Anthony Blunt were also members.

In his first term at Cambridge, Keynes received a visit from

Lytton Strachey (future author of *Eminent Victorians*) and Leonard Woolf (later husband of Virginia), two existing Apostles. Even for Keynes this visit must have seemed a little out of the ordinary and it is unlikely that he realised he was being vetted as a potential Apostle. Keynes must have made a favourable impression on his visitors as he was initiated into the Society shortly after as Apostle number 243.

Although the Apostles was supposed to be a secret society, its existence was known about throughout the University, with many more students trying but failing to become members. Its primary purpose was to discover the truth, preferably through philosophy mixed with a certain unworldliness. Indeed, this unworldliness sometimes bordered on outright rejection of the 'outside world', adding to the Apostles' aloofness. The group was also known for its homosexual tendencies around this time.

Meetings were held every Saturday at which a previously agreed topic would be discussed. It was through such meetings that Keynes was to become friends with the philosopher G E Moore (1873–1958). The Apostles was indeed a hotbed of philosophical debate, and although Moore was its leading light, the ideas of other Apostles, notably the philosophers J M E McTaggart (1866–1925) and Bertrand Russell (1872–1970), were also important in shaping Keynes's intellectual development. Keynes's own intellect was intimidating, even for the highly talented Russell. The philosopher once claimed that Keynes's mind was 'the sharpest and clearest that I have ever known. When I argued with him, I felt that I took my life in my hands, and I seldom emerged without feeling something of a fool.'[9] Nevertheless, it was Moore's *Principia Ethica* (1903), with its emphasis on truth, love and beauty and the 'good' states of mind that these produced, which was to have the greatest influence on Keynes's philosophical outlook, and in particular the importance he attached to friendship and the love of art.

With all this going on, it was no surprise that Neville Keynes was worried about his son's prospects in the Mathematics Tripos scheduled for May and June 1905. Perhaps accepting the fact that Maynard was more interested in pursuing extra-curricular activities during term time, Neville again decided to become his son's tutor, this time during the holidays. There were two other factors that Neville had to contend with if he was to see his son secure a place amongst the wranglers. First was Maynard's relaxed approach to the examinations. For example, on the penultimate day of the Tripos, Neville duly turned up at King's to check on his son only to find him still in the bath, this only 20 minutes before the exam was due to begin! Secondly, Maynard had been distracted from his studies by his love for Arthur Hobhouse, an Etonian who had just come up to Trinity. Keynes nearly fell out with Lytton Strachey over Hobhouse as they both sought the younger man's affections. Much to Keynes's disappointment, a holiday with Hobhouse in Cornwall a few weeks before the Tripos failed to produce the desired result. With this no doubt in the forefront of his mind, Keynes embarked on the Tripos on 15 May. Fears that his performance in the first few papers may have jeopardised his chances of securing a First were made up for by a stronger perform-ance towards the end. He did eventually secure a place amongst the wranglers, albeit only in 12th place, the position that Keynes himself had guessed he would achieve. This was not good enough for a fellowship at King's and, as such, Keynes had to reassess the direction he wanted his life to take. It was with this in mind that he took up the study of economics in the summer of 1905.

G E Moore (1873–1958), Professor of Philosophy at Cambridge from 1925 to 1939. As well as being the author of *Principia Ethica*, Moore, along with Bertrand Russell and others, strongly opposed the philosophical concept known as 'Idealism' which held that our knowledge of material objects, such as tables and chairs, is a product of our own ideas rather than the independent physical existence of these objects.

The India Office and Probability 1905–09

Although Keynes was a capable mathematician, it was clear that mathematics would not be the subject in which he would make his mark. Realising this and despite some initial hesitation, he turned his attention to economics. He had already made some observations on economic policy, most notably with respect to international trade: in 1903, 1904 and 1905 his speeches at the Cambridge Union had a distinctly free trade emphasis about them. Keynes combined his economic opinions with a political outlook which was decidedly anti-war and strongly in favour of Britain maintaining and strengthening its ties with the United States.

Even though he was prepared to publicly pronounce on his economic views, they were not yet supported by a solid grounding in theory. Given the dominance of Marshallian economics at Cambridge, it was somewhat inevitable that Keynes began his formal study of the subject by reading Marshall's *Principles*. This was supplemented by attendance at the great man's lectures in the autumn of 1905, weekly supervisions with Marshall and private tutoring over breakfast with Arthur Pigou (1877–1959), Marshall's protégé and his eventual successor as Professor of Political Economy at Cambridge.

As was the case with many of the things that Keynes turned his attention to, he quickly displayed an aptitude for his new subject. Most importantly, Marshall – who had tried so hard but failed to get Neville Keynes to carry his message to Oxford – quickly

Lytton Strachey *circa* 1920

saw that young Maynard had a rare talent. Writing to Neville Keynes, Marshall was fulsome in his praise: 'Your son is doing excellent work in Economics. I have told him that I should be greatly delighted if he should decide on the career of a professional economist. But of course I must not press him.'[10] Typically, Maynard was far from blind to his own abilities. In November 1905, he wrote mischievously to Strachey: *I find economics increasingly satisfactory, and I think I am rather good at it. I want to manage a railway or organise a Trust or at least swindle the investing public. It is so easy and fascinating to master the principle of these things.*[11]

Of course, learning economics was only part of Keynes's activities in Cambridge during his postgraduate year. There was also the endless round of socialising that was part of the Cambridge milieu and which Keynes had become so accustomed to. Granted, some of his best friends had left the town, most notably Strachey who was now part of the London set. These departures meant that membership of the Apostles had been significantly reduced, a situation that Keynes took it upon himself to redress. His recruitment drive resulted in only limited success. It had become difficult to find undergraduates who were tuned into the Mooreite way of interpreting the world. Of the handful of students identified for possible Apostles membership – so called 'embryos' – only two, including Lytton Strachey's younger brother James, were deemed suitable for the Society; they were inducted in early 1906.

Arthur Pigou (1877–1959) was educated at Harrow School, where he was Head Boy in 1895, and King's, where he read History. After becoming a Cambridge professor aged just 30, he volunteered for ambulance work during the First World War, an experience that transformed him from a fun, affable man into something of a recluse. His *The Economics of Welfare* (1920) is still regarded as a seminal work.

Meanwhile, it was still far from clear which career path Keynes would follow. To begin with, his relationship with Cambridge was changing. The limited success that he had at recruiting new Apostles no doubt played a part in persuading him that it was time for other challenges. Such sentiments would have been reinforced by the fact that Cambridge was, and still is, a relatively small town.

With his friends taking up residence in London, the capital's bright lights were beginning to have an increasing appeal. Of course, remaining in Cambridge was still an option. The encouragement provided by Marshall would have been enough to convince most young men to devote their life's work to the study and advancement of economics. Although he had a great deal of respect for Marshall, Keynes's rebellious streak meant that he rarely did what was expected of him. There was some talk of a legal career, but this came to nothing. Eventually, Keynes decided that a life in the service of the British government might provide an outlet for his talents and so in December 1905 he began to study for the Civil Service examinations which were to take place over two weeks in August 1906. Apart from ethics, the rest of the syllabus that candidates were to be examined on filled Keynes with dread, driven in part by boredom. Neville Keynes soon realised that his services as a tutor would again be required.

Neville's involvement did little to deter Maynard from his casual approach to examinations. He continued to take holidays, including visiting his brother Geoffrey in Germany, during which time the two brothers indulged their enthusiasm for walking and rock-climbing; extensive socialising in Cambridge; and visits to the theatre. Playing golf also continued to be high on Keynes's agenda and it was through his love of the game coupled with his friendship with fellow Etonian Daniel Macmillan that Keynes was to make the acquaintance of Daniel's younger brother Harold, the future Conservative prime minister.

In the exams themselves, Keynes's laid-back approach had little bearing on his performance. He was placed second overall out of 104 candidates with 3,498 marks out of a possible 6,000, 419 marks less than the first-placed candidate, Otto Niemeyer, a future financial controller at the British Treasury and director of the Bank of England. Keynes was left somewhat bemused. Writing to Lytton Strachey in October 1906, he complained: *My marks have arrived and left me enraged ... Knowledge seems an absolute bar to success. I have done worst in the only two subjects of which I possessed a solid knowledge – mathematics and economics. I scored more marks for English history than for mathematics – is it credible? For economics I got a relatively low percentage and was the eighth or ninth in order of merit – whereas I knew the whole of both papers in a really elaborate way. On the other hand, in political science, to which I devoted less than a fortnight in all, I was easily first of everybody. I was also first in logic and psychology and in essay.*[12] Keynes's relatively low placing in economics provoked his infamous claim that *presumably* he knew more about the subject than his examiners.

Had Keynes perhaps been a little more thorough in his preparations, he may have had a good tilt at first place which would have secured him a coveted posting at the Treasury. Had this happened, the history of economic thought would probably have been rather different. In the earliest major biography of Keynes, written in 1951 by Sir Roy Harrod, his close friend and collaborator, Harrod takes such speculation a step further by asking whether Keynes's presence at the Treasury could have helped to avert the Great Depression and whether this, in turn, might have stopped the rise of Fascism. The door to the Treasury was in fact almost open to Keynes as Niemeyer could not make his mind up: unusually, he had decided to go to the India Office but then opted for the Treasury at the last minute. Although such counterfactuals are of course intriguing, the reality was that the Civil Service examiners deemed Keynes worthy of 'only' second place and so it was that in October 1906 he began work as a clerk at the India Office.

Although Keynes spent less than two years at the Office and never actually visited India, his involvement with Indian affairs was subsequently to play an important role in helping to establish his reputation as a serious economist. It was also his first taste of Whitehall and the machinations of government. This was all well and good, but on a day-to-day basis the duties and responsibilities of a clerk were a long way from satisfying Keynes's growing appetite for hard work. Indeed, there were days when he would spend not a single minute on official matters, filling his time by working on his dissertation on Probability for a fellowship at King's.

Of course, London's bustling social scene provided some distraction, but this was not enough. After less than a year in his new job, Keynes's frustration boiled over: *I'm thoroughly sick of this place and would like to resign. Now the novelty has worn off, I am bored nine-tenths of the time and rather unreasonably irritated the other tenth whenever I can't have my own way. It's maddening to have thirty people who can reduce you to impotence when you're quite certain you are right.*[13] Given his unhappiness, it was not surprising that Keynes was soon thinking about how he could leave the Civil Service and what alternative career might be possible. A return to Cambridge was the obvious choice. But what subject? With his work on Probability going well, a life in mathematical philosophy seemed to beckon. To this end, Keynes submitted his dissertation in December 1907, confident that he would secure one of the two fellowships being offered by King's that year. The omens were certainly good. To begin with, there were only four candidates. In addition, one of the examiners was the logician W E Johnson who had been a colleague of Neville Keynes and whom Maynard had known since childhood; the other examiner was the renowned mathematician and philosopher Alfred North Whitehead.

Keynes's dissertation was an important contribution. It was the first serious attempt at developing a new theory of probability since John Venn's *The Logic of Chance* (1866). Keynes's main contention was that when examining the relationship between knowledge and probability, the subjective element had been over-emphasised to the detriment of the objective element. Put another way, knowledge is not the property of an individual but rather has a separate existence. Keynes's views received some support in Russell's *The Problems of Philosophy* which appeared in 1912 and this may have spurred Keynes to write up his own work (although the intervention of the war meant that *A Treatise on Probability* did not appear until 1921). Keynes's attack on the 'subjectivist' approach was unlikely to go unchallenged. The most serious opposition came from the brilliant young Cambridge mathematician and philosopher Frank Ramsey (1903–30) who argued that probabilities were in fact determined by the knowledge possessed by an individual. Ramsey undoubtedly got the upper hand in his dispute with Keynes and it was Ramsey's work that was to subsequently provide the foundations for the study of choice under uncertainty. Nevertheless, Keynes's ideas continued to attract supporters, most notably from the philosopher Rudolf Carnap in his 1950 *Logical Foundations of Probability*.

Back at Cambridge, it seemed that the Fellowship examiners were impressed by Keynes's work. Whitehead noted how, 'Mr Keynes' dissertation is a contribution to knowledge of great importance. It is not a mere academic exercise and, when published, will seriously affect future investigations in the subjects with which it deals. If Mr Keynes publishes much other work of this character he will attain considerable eminence as a man of science ...'[14] Underlying the dissertation was Keynes's intellectual boldness: 'Implicit in [Keynes's] argument was the view that probability should be rightly considered as the *general theory* of logic, of which deductive logic was a special case.'[15] Keynes's apparent preference for 'general' as opposed to 'special' or 'specific' theories was to be a recurring theme in his career, most keenly demonstrated with the publication of his

Frank Ramsey (1903–30) was one of the most intellectually gifted individuals of his generation. After Winchester and Trinity College, Cambridge, he was made a Fellow at King's in 1924. In a life cut tragically short by complications arising from jaundice, he made important contributions to philosophy (including the supervision of Ludwig Wittgenstein's doctoral studies at Cambridge), mathematics and economics. Keynes had a deep admiration for him.

masterpiece, *The General Theory of Employment, Interest and Money* in 1936. In so naming this work, it seems a distinct possibility that Keynes had witnessed the success of Einstein's 'general' theory of relativity and decided that a claim to generality would attract more attention.

Despite their positive signals, however, Johnson and Whitehead decided that Keynes's dissertation was not strong enough for a Fellowship, at least for that year. Much to Keynes's annoyance, the examiners attached more importance to the fact that he would be in a position to apply again the year after. Although Keynes did successfully reapply, his failure to secure a Fellowship at the first attempt was to be the only major disappointment in an otherwise glittering academic career.

Moreover, the disappointment didn't last for long. The indefatigable Marshall had continued to follow developments in Keynes's life very closely, this despite his earlier lack of success in persuading him to take up a career in economics. Now came an opportunity. During his tenure at Cambridge, Marshall had generously paid £100 towards the cost of supporting a lectureship. With his retirement rapidly approaching, Marshall took the chance of writing to Keynes, hinting that Pigou would be prepared to take on this financial burden and that Keynes would be a worthy recipient. Backed by this offer, Keynes at last decided that economics would be his life's vocation and resigned from the India Office. With Neville Keynes chairing the Economics and Politics Board, Maynard's appointment was a formality. His first lecture, entitled 'Money, Credit and Prices', was delivered on 19 January 1909.

Cambridge and Bloomsbury 1909–14

At the turn of the 20th century, economics was still finding its feet in the academic world, especially when it came to the teaching of the subject in universities. In Britain, there had been a rich tradition of eminent economists, amongst them David Ricardo, Thomas Robert Malthus and, of course, the founding father, Adam Smith. For its part, Cambridge had its professors of political economy, most notably the blind Henry Fawcett, whom Marshall had succeeded. Fawcett's teaching responsibilities were relatively small, amounting to little more than lecturing to a few 'poll men', i.e. ordinary degree students. Not surprisingly, this system produced few people of real quality. Part of the problem lay in the fact that economics did not have its own Tripos. Students had to study either Moral Science or History to get any exposure to economics. Indeed, it was through his undergraduate History degree that Pigou was first introduced to the subject. It took Marshall a full 15 years to find someone of Pigou's calibre. Marshall realised that economics would continue to be regarded by students as somehow an inferior subject as long as it was denied Tripos status and, as a result, set about campaigning in the late 1880s for the situation to be rectified. The journey was a long and hard one and it wasn't until 1903 that the authorities at Cambridge finally gave way and gave economics its own set of exams.

With the Tripos established, there were high hopes that economics would begin to attract students who would not only excel as undergraduates but may also become economics lecturers themselves, if not at Cambridge then at other British universities, thereby helping to promote Marshall's economic theories. In the early years at least, this was not to be. Perhaps most telling was the testimony of Neville Keynes, who noted how the quality of the candidates' answers in Part I of the 1907 Economics Tripos was 'poor in the extreme ... quite extraordinarily bad'.[16]

The distinct lack of good students was probably partly down to bad luck but was also influenced by the fact that the number of students enrolling to take Part I was itself still very small indeed, standing at just ten in 1905. By January 1909 the shortage of students was still worryingly apparent to the newly appointed Maynard Keynes, observing that he delivered one of his lectures *before an enormous and cosmopolitan audience – there must have been at least fifteen, I think, but a good many of them really had no business there, I am afraid, and I shall have to tell them that the lectures are not suitable to their needs* ...[17] In his own search for outstanding students, Keynes would have to wait even longer than Marshall; it was not until the second half of

Keynes described the **Reverend Thomas Robert Malthus** (1766–1834) as the first of the Cambridge economists. Keynes also identified Malthus as the first economist to highlight the importance of 'effective demand'. Keynes was of the view that many of Malthus's ideas on political economy were overshadowed by the complete domination of Ricardo's approach for a period of a hundred years and how this was a disaster for the progress of economics. Today, Malthus is most commonly associated with his 'Population Principle' which states that increases in population are geometric whilst increases in the food supply only occur on an arithmetic basis.

the 1920s that Cambridge would produce the likes of Richard Kahn (1905–89) and Joan Robinson (1903–80), the nucleus of the group that would, in the early 1930s in particular, provide crucial intellectual support at Cambridge for Keynes and his revolutionary ideas.

Notwithstanding what must have been a somewhat bleak picture at Cambridge, Keynes realised that economics was changing. Most importantly, Marshall had put it on to a more professional footing through his meticulous systematisation of both previous and new ideas. This made the process of teaching and learning easier. As a result, the number of students taking up the subject began to grow: by 1910 the number taking Part I had reached 25.

Witnessing this, Keynes decided to set up what became known as the 'Political Economy Club' in October 1909 (not to be confused with the London-based 'Political Economy Club' established by James Mill, father of John Stuart, in 1821). The Cambridge version was an informal gathering of staff and some of the best undergraduates that would meet in Keynes's rooms at King's to discuss contemporary economic issues and problems. Keynes would preside over the Club's meetings with a benevolence that encouraged students to express their opinions without fear of being made to look pretentious. At the same time, the Club could hold a certain terror for undergraduates, as one of its attendees Austin Robinson, future husband of one of Keynes's most important protégés, Joan Robinson, recalled at length: 'To the undergraduate of the early Twenties, I can say from experience, Keynes's club was fascinating but alarming. Fascinating because here one heard Keynes, a large part of the Faculty, and all the best of one's rivals discussing in realistic detail all the real and most urgent problems of the world. Alarming because if one read a paper one was likely to find one's undergraduate efforts (I speak from painful memory) being dissected by a visiting Mr. Hawtrey [an Apostle and an economist at the Treasury from 1904], destroyed by the full power of Frank Ramsey's dialectical analysis, and when one had maintained one's position to the best of one's ability for some three hours, Keynes would sum up in friendly but utterly devastating fashion – I learned a certain sympathy with the prisoner waiting for the judge's black cap.'[18] Despite this description, the Club would, over the years, become a defining feature of the economics scene at Cambridge.

With Keynes's natural sociability came a desire for the limelight. He was aware that the impact of his views was likely to be greater were he to have a higher public profile. This was a crucial lesson that Keynes had learnt from the extremely reticent Marshall. Although Marshall was well known within Cambridge, his effectiveness in influencing public opinion and government policy, while not inconsiderable, would have been significantly greater had he chosen to engage in public controversy and debate. With this in mind, Keynes's first venture into the published press was a letter to *The Economist* in February 1909, just a few weeks after his appointment at Cambridge. Consistent with his earlier views, Keynes again came out in favour of free trade, highlighting its importance in maintaining London's then role as the banking capital of the world. Keynes's first academic article was a piece entitled 'Recent Economic Events in India', which appeared in the March 1909 edition of the Cambridge-based *Economic Journal*.

Making public pronouncements would not, by themselves, establish Keynes's name as a serious economist; they had to be backed up with solid theoretical work. Thus we find Keynes jotting a note to himself in January 1909, identifying the various areas of economics upon which he set himself the task of writing down his views. Amongst other things, the note includes: papers on the Indian gold standard reserve; the riskless rate of interest and proposals for an international currency; a monograph on the theory of crises and business fluctuations; a treatise on the principles of probability; and a textbook on the principles of money. It is important to put this list in context. To begin with, it reflects Keynes's ambition. It is astonishing to think that he drew the list up only a few weeks after his appointment as a lecturer at Cambridge. The list also reflects the fact that Marshall's most important attempt to inject a greater degree of systematisation into economics had only been completed 19 years previously in the *Principles*. Keynes saw that economics was still ripe for investigation especially in the macroeconomic sphere, i.e. subjects that consider the economy as a whole, as opposed to those in the domain of microeconomics, which focus on the role of prices and the part they play in allocating scarce resources. In particular, the listing of a monograph on the theory of crises and business fluctuations, even at this early stage of Keynes's career, reflects the beginnings of an interest that would culminate in the *General Theory*.

With a growing profile at Cambridge and beyond, Keynes's career began to take greater shape in the years from 1910 to 1913. His involvement with King's deepened when he was appointed to the College's Estates Committee in 1911 and again in 1912 when he was made a fellowship elector. In this latter role, he was obliged to read fellowship dissertations relating to a whole host of topics, not necessarily connected with economics or mathematics. Nevertheless, there was some interesting reading to be had, not least a dissertation on probability submitted for consideration by the computer pioneer Alan Turing in 1935. Keynes and his fellow examiners were impressed, awarding Turing a fellowship at his first attempt.

The events that took place in the years leading up to the First World War were to play an important part in creating the platform from which Keynes could build his reputation as an economist both within the economics profession and in government. It should also be remembered that, despite his growing appetite for producing new works in economics, Keynes was still very much a Marshallian during this period.

A key aspect of the Marshallian heritage at Cambridge was the *Economic Journal*, which was, and remains to this day, the house journal of the Royal Economic Society. Aware of the fact that the *Quarterly Journal of Economics* had been founded in the US in 1886, Marshall was instrumental in founding the *Economic Journal*, the first volume of which was published in March 1891. Clearly, Marshall was of the view that a Cambridge-based journal would be a useful addition to his 'Organon' of economic analysis and would thus provide another channel for conveying his theories to other economists. Marshall's insistence on keeping mathematics out of the *Journal*'s pages meant that in the early years the articles that appeared were not particularly sophisticated; the *Journal* was certainly not the Marshallian bulldozer that Marshall had perhaps wished it to be. Of course, the *Journal* did have its moments, notably the debates regarding utility and opportunity cost that took place in 1894. However, it was really the excellent book reviews of the first editor Francis Edgeworth and later Pigou which helped to keep the *Journal* going.

By 1911, Edgeworth had been in charge for 20 years; it was time for a change. Although Pigou may have been the heir apparent, Marshall sensed that the baton had to be passed onto the younger generation if the *Journal* was to fulfil the hopes of its founders. Keynes was the obvious choice and Marshall knew it. He made a special effort to attend the October 1911 meeting of the Council of the Royal Economic Society in order to support Keynes's candidature. As a result, Keynes was a certainty and he was duly elected to the editorship, still aged only 28. He was to remain editor right up until a few months before his death.

Keynes was remarkably fair when it came to deciding what should and should not be in the *Journal*. To an extent, he had to be, not only because of his innate sense of even-handedness but also because Edgeworth had opened the first volume with the following words: 'The *Economic Journal* ... will be open to writers of different schools. The most opposite doctrines may meet here as on a fair field.' Nevertheless, Keynes found himself in a difficult position: on the one hand, he was in charge of a highly respected journal, whilst on the other, he was rapidly emerging as one of the key figures in the Cambridge School of Economics, arguably the leading school in the world at the time.

It would have been very easy for Keynes to use the *Journal* as an outlet for his own views. Granted, he did, on occasion, publish his own articles and would take the opportunity to place his comments underneath an article which he disagreed with. At the same time, Keynes would not force his ideas on others. In exchanges over proposed articles by Michal Kalecki – a man who independently discovered the principal propositions contained in Keynes's *General Theory* – there is little sign of Keynes abusing his position, this despite the fact that revisions suggested by Keynes which would have improved Kalecki's articles were rejected by the Polish economist. In the spirit of magnanimity, Keynes published the articles without his suggested revisions. When Keynes could not make his mind up about a submission or when he was concerned about the dangers of possible bias, he would consult his Cambridge colleagues, including erstwhile student and now colleague Dennis Robertson.

This is not to say that Keynes was reticent about turning down submissions where appropriate. Indeed, one of his first acts as editor was to reject a piece by the economic historian, Archdeacon Cunningham. In his typically forthright style, Keynes described Cunningham's submission as ... *the most complete wash {which} had nothing to do with economics.*[19] In the majority of cases, Keynes's judgement in deciding what should appear was correct. Nevertheless, he did make some howlers. In 1923 he rejected what would turn out to be a seminal contribution to the theory of international trade from the Swedish economist Bertil Ohlin and in 1931 refused to publish a classic article on the economics of exhaustible resources by the American economist Harold Hotelling on the grounds that it was too mathematical.

Nevertheless, Keynes's reputation was rapidly growing, not only as an economist but also as a controversialist. In the summer of 1910, he became involved in a heated exchange of views with the statistician Karl Pearson. Keynes had penned a review for the *Journal of the Royal Statistical Society*, questioning the statistical methods Pearson had employed in a study of the effects that alcoholic parents have on their children. The dispute eventually found its way into the letters page of *The Times*, with Keynes supported by Marshall and Pigou.

Meanwhile, despite a simmering rivalry between Cambridge and the London School of Economics (LSE) – a rivalry that was to hot up considerably in the 1930s – Keynes was invited to deliver a series of lectures at the LSE in May 1910 entitled 'Currency, finance and the level of prices in India'. Although he had not worked particularly hard at the India Office – at least not on Indian matters – Keynes had acquired considerable insight into the Indian economy. This, in turn, led to the publication in 1913 of his first book, *Indian Currency and Finance*, published by Macmillan, with whom Keynes had a life-long association.

Michal Kalecki (1899–1970) was arguably the greatest all-round economist of the 20th century. He made important contributions in a number of areas, including the planning of socialist economies and development economics. Recognition of his anticipation of the key concepts contained in the *General Theory* was scuppered by the fact that he published many of his early articles in Polish. Nevertheless, Joan Robinson in particular came to be a great admirer of his work. Kalecki spent time at Cambridge, Oxford and the UN. Towards the end of his career, he returned to his native Poland to work in government, but failed to have much impact.

Although he was already an economics don and editor of one of the top journals, Keynes had not yet established his name as a major economic theorist. The first step on this journey came with the appearance of *Indian Currency and Finance*. The aim of the book was to give a generally critical account of the operation of the

Indian 'Gold Standard'. India had been on a 'Silver Standard' for a large part of the 19th century. Partly because of its close trade ties with Britain, it had abandoned silver in 1898 and adopted the more commonly known Gold Standard. Under gold, a country is limited in the amount of currency it can issue according to its gold reserves. In practice, coins are issued with a fixed amount of gold in them whilst notes carry a promise of redemption in gold on the part of the issuer, which is, more often than not, a central bank. A key objective of the Gold Standard is to restrict increases in the money supply and thus prices. As far as India was concerned, Keynes was keen to stress that far from lagging behind other countries, its monetary arrangements were comparatively advanced and that it had made the right decision to adopt gold. As part of its monetary development, Keynes also urged the Indian authorities to establish a central bank, for which he provided a blueprint (although it was not until 1935 and the creation of the Reserve Bank of India that this idea came to fruition). As we shall see, Keynes would later change his mind over the effectiveness of the Gold Standard itself.

Indian Currency and Finance was far from being a bestseller, with less than a thousand copies sold in its first year. However, Keynes's skills as a careful and objective economist were becoming noticed in various quarters, as this extract from a review of the book in *The Spectator* magazine demonstrated: '[Keynes] is to be congratulated on so early an opportunity of submitting his theories to the criticisms of practised administrators and men of business, nor are his colleagues to be less congratulated on having the help of a theorist who keeps an open mind and is fully aware that monetary developments must be adapted to the habits and even to the prejudices of ordinary men ... His careful and disinterested study of the monetary facts of twenty years, and his methodical marshalling of facts and figures, will be useful even to those, and they will probably be few, who are not convinced by his reasoning.'[20] More importantly, even before its completion, *Indian Currency and Finance* had been picked up in official circles and led to Keynes's first public appointment. The Royal Commission on Indian Currency and Finance had been established by the Asquith government in April 1913 to 'inquire into and make recommendations upon the location and management of the general balances of the Government of India and related financial matters'. The Commission was headed by Austen Chamberlain, previously Chancellor of the Exchequer and a future leader of the Conservative Party.

Keynes had initially been invited to become secretary to the Commission. With the drafts of the first few chapters of *Indian Currency and Finance* further cementing his reputation in Whitehall as an expert on Indian matters, the decision was made to make him a full commission member. Keynes took up his new appointment with gusto, quickly outshining his colleagues, all of whom were pre-eminent in their own right. The fact that Keynes was the Commission's youngest member (he was just 29 when it first sat) and was in bad health for some of it (he suffered a bout of diphtheria during its proceedings) made little difference. This wasn't just youthful exuberance: the Commission accepted most of what Keynes had to say. More to the point, for significant parts of the examination of expert witnesses, Keynes was the only questioner.

When the Commission reported in early March 1914, its most important conclusion was that India should continue on the Gold Standard, a finding that was broadly supported by interested parties. Unfortunately, the outbreak of the First World War meant that the Commission's findings were shelved. Keynes's interest in Indian matters would continue for a number of years, culminating in 1919 when he appeared before the Indian Exchange and Currency Committee and again in 1926 when he was called to give evidence before the second Royal Commission

Virginia Woolf (1882–1941)

on Indian Currency and Finance. However, it was his performance as a member of the first Royal Commission which had been
vital in helping Keynes to secure a foothold in British political
and economic affairs and which would serve as the basis for his
dealings with government and civil servants for the next three
decades.

Although he was busy in Whitehall and Cambridge, Keynes

found time to deepen his social network, especially in London. The focus of this was the 'Bloomsbury Group', named after the area in Central London in which many of the so-called 'Bloomsberries' lived. The Group's origins went back to 1904 when the painter and interior designer, Vanessa Stephen (later Bell), moved herself and her three siblings Thoby, Adrian (both of whom had been at Cambridge) and Virginia Stephen (later Woolf) to 46 Gordon Square in Bloomsbury, this after the death of their father, the author and mountaineer Sir Leslie Stephen. In 1905, Vanessa founded the 'Friday Club' and Thoby his 'Thursday Evenings', informal meetings where the Stephens and their friends would discuss the arts and literature. The defining characteristic of these gatherings was the determination of the assembled crowd to reject conventional norms and beliefs in artistic and literary matters, a blast against the stuffy Victorian and early Edwardian eras. Bloomsbury quickly became known for its rebellious views. This rebellion also manifested itself in the Bloomsberries' liberal attitude towards sex. It was not uncommon for a Bloomsberry to have had intimate relations with more than one of the other members of the Group and for marriages within the Group to be 'open'.

Membership of Bloomsbury was diverse. Apart from the Stephens, other prominent figures included E M Forster, author of *A Passage to India*, Vita Sackville-West, a creator of gardens, the art critic Clive Bell, who married Vanessa Stephen in 1907, and the artists Roger Fry, a former member of the Cambridge Apostles, and Duncan Grant, a cousin of Lytton Strachey, with whom he had an affair. Keynes had been introduced to Grant in 1905 and the two embarked on their own relationship in 1908, much to Strachey's irritation. Keynes's liaison with Grant meant that he soon became a fully paid-up member of Bloomsbury, such that by 1911 both Keynes and Grant were lodging at 46 Gordon Square. Their affair did not have long to last, though, breaking down altogether in 1912.

There were various comings and goings within Bloomsbury after the First World War and the Group did manage to survive in one form or another right up to the Second World War. But the spirit of the early years was never fully recaptured. This was due to a number of factors. First was the disruption caused by the war itself. Second, death was a common theme. Lytton Strachey died in 1932 from cancer of the stomach, Roger Fry passed away in 1934 and Virginia Woolf committed suicide in 1941. Finally, key members of the Group had moved away from London, notably Vanessa Bell and Duncan Grant, who had started an affair in 1913 and moved to Charleston in the Sussex countryside in 1916.

Keynes himself gradually grew apart from the rest of the Group. Having taken on the lease of 46 Gordon Square after the First World War, he decided to become something of a country squire and in 1925 purchased Tilton, a farmhouse just down the lane from Charleston. This brought sneers from Bloomsbury as the house was packed full of modern conveniences including central heating and electric lighting. Keynes used Tilton as somewhere to rest mind and body after the exertions of London, Cambridge and overseas travel. It was also the matrimonial home that he shared with the Russian ballerina Lydia Lopokova (1892–1981) after their marriage in 1925. Later on, Bloomsbury would mock Keynes when he became Lord Keynes of Tilton in 1942.

The impact of the Bloomsbury Group on Keynes has been much debated. To begin with, Bloomsbury thrived in the limelight, although this usually stopped of directly engaging with their critics; the Group's apparent lofty detachment added to its mystery. Keynes was certainly less aloof than his fellow Bloomsberries, and he shared their desire for publicity. There is little doubt that the liberal ethos embraced by Bloomsbury appealed to the unorthodox side of Keynes's personality. The juxtaposition of Keynes as the respected Cambridge Don and political insider during the day and Keynes the bohemian in the evening is indeed a fascinating one and provides a small glimpse into the complexity of his character.

The First World War and *The Economic Consequences of the Peace* 1914–19

The outbreak of war in the summer of 1914 changed Keynes's world for good. Gone was the social, economic and political stability that he and his contemporaries had enjoyed. Keynes and Bloomsbury had railed against the norms of society, especially those associated with the Victorian era. But they had never envisaged that a world war could erupt in their lifetimes. After all, conflict on such a scale had never occurred before.

In October 1914 Keynes had returned to Cambridge for the start of the new academic year only to find the town empty of students. The war meant that the University had been robbed of a generation of undergraduates, many of whom would not return from the battlefield. Keynes summed up his feelings thus: *For myself I am absolutely and completely desolated. It is utterly unbearable to see day by day the youths going away, first to boredom and discomfort, and then to slaughter.*[21] Some of Keynes's personal friends also enlisted, including the poet Rupert Brooke, who was to die in April 1915. Brooke had been very close to Keynes's younger brother Geoffrey, after the two had met at Rugby, and it was Geoffrey who was appointed literary executor of Brooke's estate.

Feeling somewhat removed from the action, Keynes hankered after a position in government. There had already been signs that the Treasury was keen to get him on board, this after one of its senior officials Basil Blackett had consulted Keynes on a number of financial issues in August 1914. However, Keynes had to wait until early 1915 before the opportunity of a more permanent position would arise. In the opening days of January, he was made personal assistant to Sir George Paish, adviser to the then Chancellor of the Exchequer and future wartime Prime Minister, David Lloyd George. Keynes made an immediate impact. After only two weeks in the job he was appointed secretary to a Cabinet committee headed by the Liberal Prime Minister Herbert Asquith.

Despite his still relatively low salary, Keynes now found himself with a significant degree of influence. Indeed, he was now right at the heart of British politics, a place where his talents could be best employed. Unusually for a serving civil servant, Keynes was also developing a close friendship with some of his political masters, notably Herbert and Margot Asquith, with whom he would often spend weekends. Although Keynes's changing political views meant that he would fall out with the Asquiths in 1926 over the General Strike, he continued to have a lasting admiration and respect for them. Meanwhile, Keynes's work at the Treasury meant that he was often in contact with the great and the good in the City of London, and it was through such channels that Lord Cunliffe, the Governor of the Bank of England, became an acquaintance.

In March 1915 the failure of the British army to win the battle of Neuve Chapelle in northern France due to an alleged lack of shells led to Lloyd George being replaced as Chancellor by Reginald McKenna. In the subsequent fallout, Keynes became part of the

David Lloyd George (1863–1945), Liberal Chancellor of the Exchequer from 1908 to 1915, during which time he oversaw legislation introducing national insurance, and Prime Minister from 1916 to 1922. He led Britain through the second half of the First World War, but only with the support of the Conservatives in Parliament. A controversial figure, Lloyd George was often accused of underhandedness, although his sobriquet 'the Welsh Wizard' was an acknowledgment of his political brilliance.

Treasury's Finance Division, concerned specifically with Britain's financial relationships with its allies (notably France, Italy and Russia) and its borrowing and lending activities. Before he could get his teeth into his new job, illness struck again, initially in the form of appendicitis and then, more seriously, pneumonia. Keynes's life was certainly in danger at one point and it took the loving care and attention of his parents and various of his close friends to get him through. It was not until August that he was able to return to work on a full-time basis.

Meanwhile, with Britain's losses on the Western Front mounting, the question of whether to introduce conscription was forced to the top of the political agenda. Although no decision was taken in 1915, the pressure for action forced the government to introduce the first of a number of Military Service Acts in late January 1916 outlining the call-up regulations. Keynes's reaction to conscription again highlighted his complicated personality. His attitude to authority had always been somewhat mixed. On the one hand, he was a product of and very much a part of Britain's intellectual elite and all the trappings of power that went with it. As a result, he had a great deal of respect for authority. On the other hand, Keynes was also naturally rebellious; hence his membership of the Bloomsbury Group. As far as conscription was concerned, the rebellious Keynes won out. As the following draft of his application to the Tribunal dealing with exemption shows, Keynes was firm in his refusal to let his decision making be dictated by the whims of government: *I claim complete exemption because I have a conscientious objection to surrendering my liberty of judgment on so vital a question as undertaking military service. I do not say that there are not conceivable circumstances in which I should voluntarily offer myself for military service. But after having regard to all the actually existing circumstances, I am certain that it is not my duty so to offer myself, and I solemnly assert to the Tribunal that my objection to submit to authority in this matter is truly conscientious. I am not prepared on such an issue as this to surrender my right of decision, as to what is or is not my duty, to any other person, and I should think it morally wrong to do so.*[22]

The fact that he was employed at the Treasury meant that Keynes could have avoided compulsory service. He was still deeply troubled by the fact that he was working for a government which had introduced a policy which took away any freedom of choice on the part of the individual on such an important matter. In early 1916 Keynes seriously considered resigning from the Treasury; his pacifist Bloomsbury friends certainly thought that he should. In the end, he came to the conclusion that his ability to influence war policy would be maximised if he remained, albeit grudgingly, as a civil servant. At the same time, forever loyal, Keynes was instrumental in securing exemptions for a number of his friends, including Duncan Grant. Ironically, despite his non-combatant status, Keynes almost became a casualty of war in 1916. In June, the British Secretary of State for War, Lord Kitchener, set sail on the cruiser HMS *Hampshire* for diplomatic talks in Russia. Keynes had been due to travel with Kitchener's party but was withdrawn at the last moment. On reaching Scapa Flow in the Orkneys, the *Hampshire* hit a mine laid by a German U-boat. Of the 655 crew, 643 perished, Kitchener amongst them; his body was never found.

Having made the decision to stay at the Treasury, Keynes's career was soon on the up again. By early 1917, he was attending Cabinet meetings and in February was appointed head of the newly formed 'A' Division, charged solely with taking care of Britain's external financial interests, reporting directly to the new Chancellor of the Exchequer, Andrew Bonar Law. Keynes was now in charge not only of Britain's financial relations with France, Italy and Russia, but also the United States. Keynes was in a very powerful position, later observing that *all the money we either lent or borrowed passed through my hands*.[23] After having been made a Companion of the Bath (CB) in May, Keynes made his first visit

Lord Kitchener leaving the War Office on 1 June 1916, four days before he was lost in the sinking of HMS *Hampshire*. Keynes was to have been with him

to America in September as part of a mission headed by the Lord Chief Justice Lord Reading. The main objective of the trip was to strengthen Britain's financial relationship with America.

The cost of the war had put a tremendous strain on Britain. A particularly dangerous moment had occurred in late 1916 when the pound had to be propped up with emergency purchases by the investment bank J P Morgan; Britain's reserves of foreign currency were only a few days away from being wiped out completely.[24] Previous missions to America had sometimes foundered due to a lack of transparency on the part of the British as to their true financial position. As a result of Reading's honesty with the US Secretary of the Treasury William McAdoo, there was a significant improvement in bilateral relations, McAdoo agreeing to a series of loans that would see the British through to the end of the war. Although Keynes had played an important role in assisting Reading, the force of his personality arguably made a greater impact – but for all the wrong reasons. Keynes took a generally dim view of his American counterparts, driven not only by his own innate sense of superiority but also by the fact that he believed that the British, who had shouldered the main financial burden of the war since 1914, should not have to go with a begging bowl to Washington; he was to adopt a similar position 30 years later. Keynes's lack of amiability was on show for all to see: '... his haughtiness and impatience toward the Americans, which sometimes had to be restrained by his official and political seniors, gave him a reputation for rudeness that made him less effective than he might have been.'[25]

For the rest of the war, much of Keynes's time at the Treasury was taken up by further financial negotiations with the Americans. With the end of hostilities in sight, increasing attention was being paid in British and Allied circles to the peace settlement. As part of this, the question of reparations loomed large and it was to this subject that Keynes's focus gradually turned. There was still time for other pursuits. While the world waited for the Central Powers to capitulate, Keynes took the opportunity to further his artistic interests. As already noted, Keynes was attracted to Bloomsbury because it appealed to his unconventionality whilst also sharing his love of publicity. Bloomsbury was also pivotal in kindling Keynes's lifelong interest in the arts. This extended not only to providing financial support to artists – he was a co-founder of the London Artists' Association in 1925 – but also to his own activities as an art collector. His first foray took place in 1908 when he bought a drawing by the Welsh artist Augustus John, a purchase probably inspired by promptings from Duncan Grant.

With the profits from his writing and stock market investments, Keynes went on to build up a considerable collection of paintings which included pieces by Cézanne, Degas, Matisse, Picasso and Seurat. A glimpse into Keynes's sometimes playful personality is provided by the story of his purchase of Cézanne's *Apples* in March 1918. Keynes had accompanied the director of the National Gallery to Paris, the occasion of which was a sale of various paintings by the Post-Impressionists. It soon became clear that the National Gallery was not interested in anything by Cézanne and so Keynes stepped in and bought *Apples* for himself. On his return journey he decided to pay a visit to Vanessa Bell and Duncan Grant at Charleston. Anticipating the excitement his purchase would arouse, particularly with Grant, Keynes took the somewhat unusual step of leaving the painting in a hedge at the bottom of the driveway leading up to Charleston! On hearing the news that a Cézanne original was in the vicinity, Grant rushed out to find the painting, much to Keynes's delight.[26]

Whilst Keynes dabbled in the art market, his main preoccupation remained the Treasury and the imminent challenges that he and his political masters knew would be thrown up by the peace. With the warring sides finally declaring an armistice on 11 November 1918, the Allies set to work on deciding who should take responsibility for financial reparations. The big issue was to what extent Germany in particular should be made to pay for its part in the conflict. An early indication of Keynes's views on reparations came in late 1918 when he suggested that the British government should support a policy of complete cancellation of all inter-Allied war debts. This would not only be seen as a gesture of goodwill but, if accepted, would set the tone for the post-war financial talks planned to take place at the Palace of Versailles in January 1919. Total war debts between the Allies came to just under £4 billion. The net result of a complete write off would have been gains for France and Italy of £700 million and £800 million respectively. The losers would be the British, with around £900 million lost, and the United States, out of pocket by £2 billion.

Keynes was aware of the decisive military and financial role that the Americans had played in the conflict and in particular the humanitarian efforts of future US President Herbert Hoover as head of the Commission for Relief in Belgium. Keynes described Hoover as *the only man who emerged from the ordeal of Paris with an enhanced reputation.*[27] But as far as debt forgiveness was concerned, Keynes was in a minority. The Americans and the British believed that a write-off was out of the question, no doubt concerned that such a deal would encourage the Central Powers to press for an abandonment of reparations talks. The mood in certain British political quarters regarding reparations was aggressive to say the least, the most notable example being the First Lord of the Admiralty, Sir Eric Geddes, who claimed that 'I will squeeze her [Germany] until you can hear the pips squeak.'[28] With the Prime Minister Lloyd George stating in the first week of December 1918 that 'the Central Powers must pay the cost of the war up to the limit of their capacity'[29] – this pronouncement no doubt influenced by the British general election which was scheduled for 14 December – it was no surprise that reparations became the most important issue at Paris.

Despite what to the British government must have been his unsettling suggestions on debt, Keynes was appointed the Treasury's official representative at the peace talks. He was also the Chancellor of the Exchequer's deputy on the Supreme Economic Council. The setting for the negotiations was the imposing Hall of Mirrors. The opening session was held on 18 January 1919 with delegates from 26 countries in attendance. Given the large number of nations involved, it was decided that the more important decisions would be taken by a council made up of France, Britain and the United States. The respective leaders of these nations were Prime Minister Georges Clemenceau, Prime Minister David Lloyd George and President Woodrow Wilson.

With the Allies in no mood for compromise, the writing

was already on the wall for the defeated; the exclusion from the talks of Germany and Austria-Hungary only reinforced this feeling. Keynes became increasingly frustrated by the direction in which the negotiations were going, a frustration compounded by physical exhaustion. After much to-ing and fro-ing, the Allies reached a final agreement which was issued to Germany on 7 May. It demanded that Germany should give up a significant amount of its existing territory to neighbouring countries, restrict the size of its military, and pay substantial damages to the Allies. After some initial protestations, the Germans agreed to the conditions and signed the Treaty of Versailles on 28 June 1919. Keynes had also already seen what was coming and was disgusted by it. He hung on as long as possible, but by early June the pressure had grown to bursting point. Keynes wrote to Lloyd George that the *battle is lost* and that he was *slipping away from this scene of nightmare. I can do no more good here*.[30] He had resigned from the British delegation.

Keynes was not the only delegate at Paris who had advocated forgiveness. However, his seniority and the dramatic act of his resignation meant that many questions were asked about the nature of the settlement. After a few weeks of reflection back in England, Keynes decided that he could not let the matter drop. Although the Treaty had already been signed, Keynes sat down to pen what would become a major attack on the Allies. The result was *The Economic Consequences of the Peace*, a book which would make him known the world over.

Keynes began writing *The Economic Consequences* in the peace and quiet of Charleston in late June 1919. Within a few short months the book was ready. By the time it appeared in December, Keynes had already returned to his lecturing duties at Cambridge. By publishing such a controversial piece, he knew that he would be putting his already considerable reputation at risk. This was undoubtedly one of those times when, Keynes was 'in addition to being a publicist ... was also an economist'.[31] His protests also indicated his willingness to jeopardise the informal political power base that he had been nurturing, thus underlining his status as something of an 'establishment maverick'. Publication went ahead as planned and the impact was immediate. In its first two months, *The Economic Consequences* sold nearly 85,000 copies and was translated into 11 languages. Fortunately for Keynes, profits from the book were enough to help him cover the losses he had suffered on the stock market.

The Economic Consequences of the Peace is justly famous for two reasons, first, because of its technical critique of the reparations chapter of the Treaty of Versailles, and second, because of its vivid personal characterisations of Clemenceau, Lloyd George and Wilson. With respect to reparations, Keynes calculated that Germany could only afford to pay up to £2 billion to the Allies and that even this was a relatively optimistic estimate. It was also significantly less than the amount of money being demanded by the Allies: in 1921 the Inter-Allied Reparations Commission finally set the total reparations figure for all the Central Powers at nearly £24 billion. Under the terms of the Commission's proposals, it would have taken Germany until 1984 to pay off its share of reparations. Keynes was concerned that the Allies' determination to decapitate the economies of the defeated nations and of Germany in particular – Keynes famously labelled the Allies' approach as a *Carthaginian peace* – would result in the impoverishment of Europe: *{The Allies} have run the risk of completing the ruin which Germany began, by a peace which, if it is carried into effect, must impair yet further, when it might have restored, the delicate, complicated organisation, already shaken and broken by war, through which alone the European peoples can employ themselves and live.*[32]

Keynes claimed that the Allied powers had done nothing to create greater political and social stability in Central Europe and had lost the opportunity to integrate Russia more fully into the European family of nations. Granted, some progress had been made on strengthening territorial integrity in Europe. Most importantly, the charter of the League of Nations was included in the Treaty of Versailles. The proposal to create a League of Nations (the forerunner to today's United Nations) was the last of the 'Fourteen Points' outlined by President Wilson in January 1918; Wilson would receive the Nobel Peace Prize in 1919 for his wartime efforts. Nevertheless, the reparations issue continued to be the source of much controversy long after the delegates at Versailles had returned home.

The term 'Carthaginian peace' derives from the three Punic Wars fought between Rome and Carthage, the first in 264 AB and the last in 146 AB. After having successfully captured Carthage in the third and final conflict, Rome killed its inhabitants and destroyed its infrastructure, making Carthage virtually uninhabitable. Since then, a 'Carthaginian peace' has come to refer to a situation where the loser in a war is completely subjugated by the victor, often to an unnecessary and cruel extent.

Keynes's second line of attack was his description of the 'Big Three' leaders at Versailles. Over the years, these portrayals have arguably received as much attention as the technical analysis contained in *The Economic Conse-quences*. Keynes's decision to get personal was influenced in large part by the irreverence of Bloomsbury; Lytton Strachey's *Eminent Victorians* was no doubt a model for Keynes.

It would be unfair to assume that Keynes's descriptions of the Big Three were all negative. Indeed, he went out of his way to highlight some of their more appealing features. But Keynes followed this up with devastating tirades. Describing Clemenceau, Keynes noted how: *{He} was by far the most eminent {of the three}, and he had taken the measure of his colleagues. He alone both had an idea and had considered it in all its consequences. His age, his character, his wit, and his appearance joined to give him objectivity and a defined outline in an environment of confusion.*[33] Before the reader's mind is convinced by Keynes's words, this follows: *But speech and passion were not*

(*Left to right*) Clemenceau, Wilson and Lloyd George at the Versailles Conference

lacking when they were wanted, and the sudden outburst of words, often followed by a fit of deep coughing from the chest, produced their impression rather by force and surprise than by persuasion.[34] In a brilliant turn of phrase, Keynes concluded that Clemenceau *had one illusion – France; and one disillusion – mankind, including Frenchmen, and his colleagues not least.*[35]

Keynes had a changeable relationship with Lloyd George. Although the two men enjoyed closer ties in the 1920s as their respective economic views became more aligned, Keynes's closeness to the Asquiths meant that he was not on the best of terms with Lloyd George in the period leading up to Versailles. Just after the conference, Keynes described Lloyd George as a *goat-footed bard, this half-human visitor to our age from the hag-ridden magic and enchanted woods of Celtic antiquity.*[36] Even if Keynes was impressed by Lloyd George's seemingly super-human powers of insight and intuition, he ultimately saw 'the goat' as something of a schemer: *To see the British Prime Minister watching the company, with six or seven senses not available to ordinary men, judging character, motive, and subconscious impulse, perceiving what each was thinking and even what each was going to say next, and compounding with telepathic instinct the argument or appeal best suited to the vanity, weakness, or self-interest of his immediate auditor, was to realise that the poor President {Wilson} would be playing blind man's buff in that party.*[37]

Keynes's treatment of President Wilson was just as stinging, perhaps more so. Keynes saw in Wilson a man genuinely interested in creating peace and stability in Europe and to do what was *just and right* at Versailles. He was also impressed by Wilson's physical presence: *His head and features were finely cut and exactly like his photographs, and the muscles of his neck and the carriage of his head were distinguished.*[38] The compliments stopped there: *But, like Odysseus, the President looked wiser when he was seated; and his hands, though capable and fairly strong, were wanting in sensitiveness and finesse ... But more serious than this, he was not only insensitive to his surroundings in the external sense, he was not sensitive to his environment at all. What chance could such a man have against Mr Lloyd George's unerring, almost medium-like, sensibility to everyone immediately round him? ... {T}his blind and deaf Don Quixote was entering a cavern where the swift and glittering blade was in the hands of the adversary ... There can seldom have been a statesman of the first rank more incompetent than the President in the agilities of the council chamber.*[39]

Was Keynes being unfair? In their defence, both Wilson and Clemenceau were in poor health at Versailles, with Clemenceau only narrowly surviving an assassin's bullet on 19 February 1919. Both men would be dead within a few years, Wilson in 1924 after suffering a stroke in October 1919 brought on by efforts to establish the League of Nations, and Clemenceau in 1929 from natural causes. Had they been physically fitter, the outcome of the Paris talks and thus Keynes's caricaturing may have been different. As already noted, Keynes had mixed feelings towards Lloyd George. Nevertheless, he viewed Lloyd George with a significant degree of scepticism, despite the Welshman's famed political nous. Even though there was a rapprochement later on, any lasting friendship was doomed after Lloyd George's fury at Keynes's depiction of him in *Essays in Biography* which appeared in 1933.

As for *The Economic Consequences* itself, it not surprisingly created a tremendous reaction, both positive and negative. The initial reception was broadly positive, driven more by the fact that nobody seemed capable of refuting Keynes's economic arguments and by a preoccupation with his dazzling depictions of the Big Three, this at the expense of the deeper analysis that could have been made of the reparations issue. Less positively, Keynes was accused in many quarters of being politically naïve (an interesting insight when considered alongside the fact that Keynes did not pursue a political career himself despite a number of opportunities and the promise of high office); having pro-German sympathies; being anti-French; and of writing a book that created so much guilt amongst the British and French political elite that it contributed to their failure to properly address the issue of Germany's rearmament in the 1930s under Hitler. Keynes attempted to answer a number of these points in *A Revision of the Treaty* which appeared in January 1922.

However, it was to be another quarter of a century before the most telling criticism of *The Economic Consequences* appeared, with the publication in 1946 of *The Carthaginian Peace, or the Economic Consequences of Mr. Keynes*. The author was Étienne Mantoux, a French economist who had penned his reply to Keynes in 1944 but did not live long enough to see its publication after being killed fighting for the Free French Forces just eight days before the end of the Second World War.

Mantoux already had an association with Versailles (albeit indirectly) as his father Paul had been Clemenceau's interpreter at the talks. Unlike his previous critics, Mantoux focused on Keynes's claim that Germany could not afford to pay the full cost of reparations as its economy had been shattered by war. Through painstaking and detailed analysis, Mantoux showed that many of Keynes's prophecies turned out to be wrong. The most startling evidence came from Germany's iron and steel industries, which Keynes predicted would suffer contractions in output in the years following the war. In fact, by 1927 output had grown by around a third compared to 1913. Keynes was also wide of the mark in regard to German coal production and the country's level of national savings in the post-war period.[40] Most chilling was the fact that Germany had the financial and physical capacity to embark on a massive rearmament programme and thus was probably in a better position to afford reparations than Keynes had claimed. In the end, Germany paid only one-eighth of the total reparations sought by the Allies.

In spite of all the controversy that surrounded *The Economic Consequences*, there is no doubt that it made Keynes a household name overnight both in Britain, the United States and the rest of the world. The book also brought into sharp focus Keynes's relationship with his former employer, the Treasury. There are varying opinions as to the extent to which Keynes burned his bridges with officialdom as a result of publishing *The Economic Consequences*. It is probably fair to say that his influence in government was much reduced in the years after Versailles. The fact that he was no longer employed by the Treasury of course didn't help. At the same time, Keynes was far from being 'in the wilderness':[41] it was only a few months after the appearance of *The Economic Consequences* that the government was sounding him out for his views on monetary policy and solutions to unemployment. Although it may be pushing matters to argue that Keynes had 'never left the Treasury',[42] it was difficult for the Treasury mandarins to ignore his advice in the years following Versailles.

Man of Action 1919–31

Keynes's experience at Versailles had made him wary of the political process and his ability to influence it. Although the Treasury continued to consult him on various matters, it was clear that a return to Whitehall in an official capacity would not be on the agenda, at least for a few years. Keynes was also still eager to make his name as a top-flight economic theorist. *Indian Currency and Finance* had brought him to the attention of his fellow economists as well as government. Despite the fact that the book was and continues to be regarded as a landmark study of the Indian banking system, it was far from being the groundbreaking theoretical analysis that would have propelled Keynes into the first rank of his chosen profession. Moreover, the controversy that had surrounded *The Economic Consequences of the Peace* and the accusations against Keynes that he was more interested in propaganda than objectivity spurred him to devoting much of the 1920s (partly in vain as it turned out, at least in his view) and the first half of the 1930s (a somewhat more successful period) to purely theoretical matters and, with it, the bulldozing of some of the old orthodoxies.

When Keynes returned to Cambridge for the Michaelmas Term in October 1919, his duties as an economics lecturer had changed significantly. In particular, his teaching responsibilities were much reduced. Immediately before the war, he was sometimes lecturing for up to seven hours a week on subjects including 'The Stock Exchange and the Money Market', 'The Theory of Money',

'Currency and Banking' and 'The Principles of Economics'. The fact that economics now had its own Tripos meant that there were a number of talented students coming through the system who could become lecturers and were thus able to take some of the teaching load off their seniors, Keynes included. Indeed, immediately after the war, Keynes's share of lecturing was 'very limited ... seldom more than some eight, remarkably inspiring, lectures in any one year, concerned with problems at which he was himself working'.[43] Keynes's willingness to share his latest thoughts with his students was a recurring theme throughout his career and was a manifestation of the closely-knit college life that is encouraged at Cambridge.

Meanwhile, Keynes's personality went through some significant changes during the 1920s. He was always sympathetic towards students, especially those who were willing to expose themselves to the sharply concentrated intellectual discussion that characterised the Political Economy Club. But matters were quite different when it came to his contemporaries at Cambridge. When he didn't agree with their opinions, Keynes's view was that they *should know better*, an attitude that sometimes spilled over into intolerance. This was particularly apparent during the early 1920s and may have partly reflected the hangover of disappointment and anger that Keynes suffered as a result of his experiences at Versailles. The dissipation of this irritation as the 1920s wore on provides some support for this view.

Keynes would also have been concerned about his financial position. His was already a reasonably wealthy middle-class family. Keynes's grandfather John Keynes had been a successful businessman, and Maynard was keen to make an even greater fortune. Some money (albeit rather limited) was to be made from teaching and supervising and, as *The Economic Consequences* demonstrated, from publishing; Keynes also derived an income from journalism and from his appointment to the board of the National

Mutual Life Assurance Company in 1919, and his promotion to chairman, still aged only 38, in 1921. But it was through stock market speculation that he believed a substantial fortune could be made.

Even from a relatively early age, Keynes seems to have been attracted by the thrill of making money from the comfort of his armchair, investing nearly £170 in the Marine Insurance Company in July 1905. After many years of dabbling, his departure from the Treasury in 1919 was the trigger for a significant ramping up in his share and commodity dealing activities. Believing that the financial clout of a syndicate of investors would be more effective in turning a profit, Keynes decided to team up with O T Falk, one of his ex-colleagues at the Treasury, who since leaving government service had landed a job as a partner at a major London stockbroker. The group's initial capital sum was £30,000 and contributing investors included a number of Keynes's direct family and Duncan Grant. The first investment, a bet on the movement of the French franc and the Indian rupee, was made in January 1920. Initially, the venture was quite successful, but by May of that year, adverse currency movements had wiped out any profits and almost resulted in Keynes's bankruptcy.

His subsequent career as an investor is worth considering a little further here as it had a significant impact not only on his own life and work but also changed the fortunes of King's College. Forever the optimist, Keynes's did not let the syndicate experience deter him from getting back into the market. Over the next couple of years, his wealth recovered greatly, such that by 1924 his net assets stood at just under £64,000. Market downturns and an element of overexposure meant that there were losses in 1929 and again in 1937–8 and 1940. However, by the end of the Second World War, Keynes's confidence in the ability of the market to rebound meant that his net asset position stood at over £400,000.[44]

Apart from helping to expand his art collection, stock market profits opened up a number of other avenues for Keynes. To begin with, it fed into his theoretical work. Keynes was one of the few economists at that time to have had any direct experience of the financial markets. He turned this to his advantage, using it to inform his writing on the theory of futures contracts. As early as 1923 Keynes had already coined the term 'backwardation', well known to modern-day students of finance to refer to the situation in futures markets where the price of a contract falls the closer the contract gets to expiry.

At a more practical level, Keynes was able to purchase a country pile at Tilton in 1925. After Cambridge, Tilton was Keynes's favourite place. It enabled him to indulge his enthusiasm for long walks and gave him the peace with which to get on with his theoretical and governmental work. However, Tilton was hardly a social desert. In keeping with the spirit of Bloomsbury, there were regular visitors: not only were Vanessa Bell and Duncan Grant nearby at Charleston but also Leonard and Virginia Woolf lived just a few miles away in Rodmell. Keynes also liked to invite some of his closest colleagues down to Tilton for the weekend to discuss matters of theory. Richard Kahn, Keynes's favourite pupil and later on his most trusted confidante, was a regular visitor. The two men could often be found debating economics whilst picking vegetables in the garden.

Then there was King's College. Keynes's interest in College finances had begun in 1909 when he was made an Inspector of Accounts and 1911 with his elevation to the Estates Committee. But it was with his appointment as Second Bursar in late 1919 and then as First Bursar in 1924 (a post that he retained right up until his death) that Keynes became more seriously involved. From the beginning, the College gave Keynes extensive leeway in investing its money. In June 1920 he was given permission to invest £30,000 in foreign government securities. As well as investments in equities and commodities, Keynes also involved the College in property transactions. Many of these were sales, although there were some acquisitions, such as the purchase of farmland in Lincolnshire in 1925.[45]

Of course, things did not always go to plan. In one amusing incident in 1936, Keynes purchased the equivalent of one month's wheat consumption in Britain with a view to turning a quick profit. A problem arose as the wheat was bought on a futures contract and so had to be delivered on a certain date. Realising the massive storage problem that would ensue if the wheat was in fact delivered, Keynes took the somewhat unusual step of calculating the cubic capacity of the world-famous chapel at King's College to see if it would be big enough to cater for the upcoming delivery, only to find that it was too small. Ultimately, Keynes ingeniously wriggled out of his predicament by claiming that the wheat had to be cleaned before delivery could take place. This gave him the breathing space in which to resell the wheat back into the market.[46] These anecdotes aside, Keynes was a spectacularly successful First Bursar, increasing the College's capital many times over during his bursarship.

Although he had returned to academia, Keynes was still a keen observer of the international economic environment and was searching for new outlets for his thoughts. In March 1923 he was one of a group of investors and intellectuals who took over the *Nation and Athenaeum*, a magazine with Liberal sympathies; in 1931 it merged with the *New Statesman*. Keynes would often use the pages of the *Nation and Athenaeum* to expound on various subjects including his views on Russia and to answer the question 'Am I a Liberal?'.

Meanwhile, the world economy was still reeling in the aftermath of the First World War. Although there had been some signs of recovery, depression struck in 1921, caused in part by an upward shift in US interest rates. In response, representatives from 34 nations met in Genoa, Italy, in April-May 1922 to discuss how their economies could be stabilised. C P Scott, the legendary owner and editor of the *Manchester Guardian* (forerunner of *The Guardian*), was on the look out for someone who could both report on the conference's proceedings whilst also providing incisive opinion; Keynes was the perfect man for the job. Scott commissioned Keynes to put together a series of supplements under the general title 'Reconstruction in Europe' which appeared between April 1922 and January 1923.

The main outcome of the Genoa talks was a recommendation that there should be a general return to the Gold Standard. Britain had adopted gold back in 1821 as a result of, on the one hand, a significant silver shortage that had occurred during the Napoleonic Wars and, on the other hand, because of the gold rushes in the US in the middle part of the 19th century which had triggered a major expansion in the gold supply and America's own adoption of the Gold Standard in 1873. However, gold was abandoned on the outbreak of hostilities in 1914 as the combatants were forced to print large sums of money in order to more easily finance the war effort. Not surprisingly, the conflict caused a massive disruption of international trade and the central bankers at Genoa believed that the re-adoption of the Gold Standard would be the only way to normalise trade patterns.

Having reported on the goings-on at Genoa, Keynes began to draw together his thoughts on post-war monetary arrangements. These appeared in *A Tract on Monetary Reform* which was published in December 1923 and which some, notably the great monetarist Milton Friedman (1912–2006), consider to be Keynes's best book. Its basic premise is that money is the most important variable in the economy: if it can be controlled, then policy-makers have a much better chance of controlling all of the other variables that help to determine levels and changes in economic activity.

This view of the primary importance of money – a view which, incidentally, Keynes would come to question in the 1930s – is based on the famous 'quantity theory of money', the oldest idea in economics. In fact, one of the earliest references to the quantity theory is made by Copernicus, writing as early as the 16th century. The theory states that changes in prices are directly related to changes in the money supply. Thus if the money supply is doubled, then according to the theory prices will also double. In *A Tract on Monetary Reform*, Keynes gave a large measure of support to the quantity theory, which at the time was considered an essential part of economic orthodoxy. At the beginning of the book's third chapter, Keynes states how the theory is *fundamental* and how its correspondence with the facts is *not open to question*. In a famous passage, Keynes goes on to point out however that although the exactness of the direct relationship between changes in the money supply and prices may not be open to question in the long run, the long run is *a misleading guide to current affairs*. In the long run *we are all dead. Economists set themselves too easy, too useless a task if in tempestuous seasons they can only tell us that when the storm is long past the ocean is flat again.*[47] Keynes clearly had some doubts about the quantity theory, even if he wasn't yet in a position to provide an alternative theoretical apparatus of how the economy worked.

Discussions about the Gold Standard continued well after Genoa, as did the debate about the effectiveness of manipulating the money supply as a means of controlling inflation. Interest in the latter issue was compounded by the occurrence of hyperinflation in Germany in 1923 which had been triggered by a flood of new money that the government had pumped into the economy. To put what was happening into some kind of context, it is worth considering that there were just 6 billion marks in circulation in Germany in 1913. By the end of October 1923, hyperinflation meant that the price of a kilo of rye bread had rocketed to a staggering 5½ billion marks; a few weeks later the price had escalated further to an incomprehensible 428 billion marks.[48] Against this background, it was not unusual for workers to be paid not only every day but two or three times a day. Although Britain did not have an inflation problem in the early 1920s, the deflation that had set in after the boom of the immediate post-war years was causing just as much concern. Calls for the return of the Gold Standard grew ever louder. The Chancellor of the Exchequer at the time was one Winston Churchill. Keynes knew Churchill well. The two men were members of the Other Club, a dining and gambling clique. Keynes would use the Club to ply Churchill with his latest thoughts and theories. He even won £10 off the future war leader on the outcome of the May 1929 General Election!

However, when it came to the question of whether Britain should return to gold, Keynes failed to convince Churchill that the more active management of the pound would be preferable. So it was in April 1925 that Britain again adopted the Gold Standard. From the beginning, it was clear that Churchill had made what he would later acknowledge to be one of his worst decisions as a politician. The fatal error lay in the fact that the pound's value against the US dollar was kept at its pre-war rate of US$4.86, an overvaluation of around 10 per cent. The result was disastrous: exporters suffered considerably, notably the coal industry, and it was attempts to cut the wages of miners in order to improve competitiveness that was the catalyst for the General Strike of 1926. Frustrated, Keynes set out his position in three articles in the *Evening Standard* in July 1925. Shortly after, the Hogarth Press (owned and run by Leonard and Virginia Woolf) turned the articles into a pamphlet entitled *The Economic Consequences of Mr Churchill*. Keynes was eventually proved right: although it took six years, the pound's strength meant that the pressure on exporters grew intolerable and Britain was forced off gold in September 1931.

Whilst Keynes continued to pursue his professional career, his personal life was showing signs of change. He was a keen watcher and patron of the ballet, an interest which, in later life, led to him becoming the Treasurer of the Camargo Ballet Society. In late 1918 he had been introduced to the ballerina Lydia Lopokova. Lydia came from a relatively humble background, her father having been a theatre usher in St Petersburg. Nevertheless, she and her three siblings all became ballet dancers, with Lydia headlining with Diaghilev's world-famous Ballets Russes; Nijinksy had been one of her dancing partners.

Keynes was fascinated by Lydia's unconventionality and the amusing broken English she spoke. As a relationship between the two developed, Lydia received a mixed reception from Keynes's family and friends. Keynes's mother, Florence, got on famously with Lydia, Florence no doubt relieved that her eldest son had at last decided to settle down. Bloomsbury reacted differently. Many of the Bloomsberries viewed their group as a closed shop, something of a fortress. Vanessa Bell wrote to Keynes: 'Clive [Bell] says he thinks it is impossible for any one of us ... to introduce a new wife or husband into the existing circle ... We feel that *no one* can come into the sort of intimate society we have without altering it.'[49] Bloomsbury never quite came to terms with Lydia, whom they tended to look down on as someone who could never aspire to their own dizzying intellectual heights. Despite his fondness for Bloomsbury, Keynes was not swayed and in August 1925 he married Lydia at St Pancras Registry Office.

Leonard and Virginia Woolf founded the Hogarth Press in Richmond, London in 1917. In its early days it was a private press and it was in this capacity that it published the first UK book edition of T S Eliot's poem, *The Waste Land*, in September 1923, the task of typesetting being performed by Virginia herself. Hogarth's growing success led to it being put on to a more commercial footing after the Second World War.

Given his previous health problems, his growing wealth and the distractions of marriage, Keynes's might have been expected to reduce his workload. However, he had by this time become a workaholic and could not resist becoming involved in anything

Lydia and Keynes on their wedding day

that held even a tangential interest. There was some give and take. Thus in early 1927 he resigned from the *Chinese torture* of the Cambridge University Council and in January 1928 turned down an offer from the Cambridge University Liberals to stand as their candidate in the General Election of May 1929. Keynes already had a packed life. His activities from the mid-1920s up until the end of 1930 can be broadly divided into two: on the one hand, he was *becoming fashionable again* in Whitehall, helped by what turned out to be his correct foretelling of the failure of the Gold Standard. He also continued to be heavily involved in writing, both for the popular press and academically. A number of pieces poured forth from his pen during this period, including *The End of Laissez-Faire* in July 1926. Meanwhile, in his role as editor of the *Economic Journal*, Keynes played a key part in a heated debate in the *Journal*'s pages – as did the Swedish economist Bertil Ohlin – in 1929 over the economic effects that reparations had on both donor and recipient countries, the so-called 'German Transfer Problem'. This became one of the most famous controversies in economics. Years later in 1952, the celebrated American economic theorist Paul Samuelson proved that Keynes's position on the matter was, under given conditions, correct.

Keynes's ideas on how the economy worked were forever changing, hence his much-misquoted comment *When someone persuades me that I am wrong, I change my mind. What do you do, sir?* It was also apparent that the Cambridge economic heritage which had been rejuvenated by Marshall had once again become somewhat neglected. Part of the problem was with A C Pigou, Marshall's successor as Professor of Political Economy. Pigou, or 'The Prof' as Keynes called him, was a devout Marshallian, once claiming that 'It's all in Marshall'. Of course, Pigou himself had made a number of important contributions to economic theory and is to this day regarded as the father of welfare economics. However, he was by nature something of a recluse and hated the thought of having to take on any administrative duties. After 1920 his theoretical offerings began to dry up. Cambridge needed another Marshall, another innovator. Keynes's *A Tract on Monetary Reform* was certainly impressive, but it still reflected his Marshallian heritage.

With this in mind, Keynes embarked on a new, much more technical book in November 1924. What with all his other commitments, Keynes's work on what was supposed to be his *magnum opus* was constantly interrupted, even though he now had his refuge at Tilton. 'By the end of 1928 the complaints of tiredness [grew] more insistent', the result being that various parts of the book were left 'mouldering for months unread at Tilton'.[50] *A Treatise on Money* would not indeed appear until October 1930. What did Keynes attempt to do in the *Treatise*? The aim was to *discover the dynamical laws governing the passage of a monetary system from one position of equilibrium to another*.[51] Keynes touched upon ideas that he would develop more fully in *The General Theory*, including his 'liquidity preference' theory, i.e. the extent to which individuals prefer to hold their money in the form of cash as opposed to other forms of wealth, and his view that the business cycle is mainly driven by fluctuations in investment which are, in turn, heavily dependent on business confidence, or *animal spirits* to use Keynes's terminology. However, it is highly questionable whether Keynes really succeeded in achieving what he had set out to do. A major problem was that his analysis was still heavily focused on the role that changes in prices play in the business cycle as opposed to changes in output; this intuitive leap would have to wait until *The General Theory*.

What was Keynes's own opinion of the *Treatise*? Writing to his mother shortly before it was published, Keynes sounded a note of relief that the book was finally out of his hands but also disappointment that it had not lived up to his expectations: *This evening, at last, I have finished my book.... {O}ne parts from it with mixed feelings.... Artistically it is {a} failure – I have changed my mind too much during the course of it for it to be a proper unity*.[52] Keynes's view that the *Treatise* was a 'failure' is something of an exaggeration. True, it did not have the revolutionary impact he may have hoped for it. The *Treatise* should instead be seen as part of Keynes's transition as an economist. Keynes himself acknowledged this: *The ideas with which I have finished up are widely different from those with which I began. The result is, I am afraid, that there is a good deal in this book which represents the process of getting rid of the ideas which I used to have and of finding my way to those which I now have. There are many skins which I have sloughed still littering these pages.*[53] The line of evolution in Keynes's thinking was beginning to form, started as it had been by the heavily Marshallian *A Tract on Monetary Reform* and now progressing through *A Treatise on Money*. The final stage in the process would have to wait until 1936 and the distinctly un-Marshallian *General Theory*.

Back in the political world, the Labour government returned under Ramsay MacDonald in May 1929 was becoming increasingly concerned about economic instability. Most tellingly, the rate of unemployment during the 1920s had been much higher than ever before. Desperate for answers, MacDonald appointed a Royal Commission on Finance and Industry in November 1929 headed by a Scottish judge, Hugh Macmillan. The Commission's remit was to 'inquire into banking, finance and credit, paying regard to the factors both internal and international which govern their operation, and to make recommendations calculated to enable these agencies to promote the development of trade and commerce and the employment of labour'.[54] With Keynes's star again in the ascendant, he was invited and accepted a position on the Commission. He joined an illustrious cast: apart from Keynes, other members included the former Chancellor of the Exchequer and then head of the Midland Bank, Reginald McKenna, and the then head of the Transport and General Workers' Union and future Foreign Secretary, Ernest Bevin. An Economic Advisory Council (EAC) was established to support the work of the main committee.

Although it met on dozens of occasions, the Commission, and with it the EAC, was a source of frustration for Keynes. With the onset of the economic downturn in late 1929 and early 1930 that was to grow into the Great Depression, Keynes felt that the appointment of a small group of professional economists was required in order to properly examine its causes and draw up practical solutions. Keynes even had an idea as to who such economists should be. In July 1930 he wrote to MacDonald; *May I indicate the sort of membership which I have in mind: Sir Josiah Stamp, Mr H.D. Henderson and myself, as representing the Economic Advisory Council; Professor Henry Clay as representing the Bank of England's new organisation for dealing with rationalisation; Professor Pigou of Cambridge, Professor L. Robbins of London, and Mr D.H. Robertson, as leading academic economists.*[55]

MacDonald promptly followed Keynes's advice and the 'Committee of Economists' held its first meeting on 10 September 1930; Keynes assumed the chairmanship. Despite his initial optimism, the Committee also proved to be something of a mixed blessing for Keynes. He had demonstrated his institutional power by getting it established in the first place, with all of the personnel he had recommended to MacDonald in attendance and with Richard Kahn acting as its joint secretary. On the other hand, the Committee's deliberations, as it turned out, were often characterised by dissent. The most notable instance of this was Lionel Robbins's opposition to a proposal supported by the other members to introduce an emergency import tariff. After some tense exchanges between Keynes and Robbins, Robbins was allowed to set out his own position in a minority report.

In addition to internal dissent, the Committee's main report ended up being buried by the Cabinet as it was allegedly too inconclusive to be of any practical use. This abandonment highlighted the fact that Keynes's institutional influence during this period may not, in fact, have been as great as he would have wished, despite his own belief just a few years beforehand that his ideas were beginning to be taken more seriously in official circles.

Finally, the views that Keynes had expressed on the Committee of Economists were very much in line with those he had developed in the *Treatise*. However, the onset of the Great Depression changed everything. Unemployment in Britain had increased to over 20 per cent in 1931. Only a few months after the *Treatise* had appeared, Keynes came to the conclusion that his description of the causes of business fluctuations was faulty and that it could not provide a coherent explanation for the growing unemployment problem. With this in mind, Keynes set out on the long and winding road that would eventually lead to *The General Theory*.

Revolutionising Economics 1931–6

In May 1931 Keynes visited the United States. During his trip he made a quick courtesy call on President Hoover at the White House before returning to England in July. The main purpose of his visit was to deliver three lectures at the Harris Foundation in Chicago on the 'Economic Analysis of Unemployment'. Keynes still used the apparatus contained in the *Treatise* as the focus for his lectures, although his emancipation from its strictures had already begun. At the beginning of the year, a gifted group of young Cambridge economists held regular meetings to discuss the *Treatise*. Their insights and criticisms were to play an important part in Keynes's liberation from his old Marshallian ways.

Keynes's reputation as an economist and as a man who could influence opinion was at a relatively low ebb in 1931. Keynes himself was well aware of his own failings. He opened his *Essays in Persuasion* with the words, *Here are collected the croakings of twelve years – the croakings of a Cassandra who could never influence the course of events in time.*[56] This impotence was driven in particular by Churchill's decision to return Britain to the Gold Standard in 1925 against Keynes's advice, the overly technical analysis of the *Treatise*, and the ditching by the government of the Committee of Economists' report.

Keynes was now faced with a new frustration, that of explaining how unemployment had reached such a high level. The existing body of economic theory, founded on the ideas of the so-called 'Classical' economists, really had no coherent explanation for it, this despite the many illustrious names associated with that school, including Adam Smith, David Ricardo and John Stuart Mill; Keynes also placed Marshall and Pigou in the classical mould. For this group of thinkers, the causes of unemployment were relatively straightforward: they viewed it simply as the result of either frictions in the labour market, i.e. the time it takes for a newly laid-off worker to find a new job, or due to money wages being too 'sticky' or resistant to change. Money (or nominal) wages do not take into account the effects of inflation, whereas real wages do. Wage stickiness can be the result of various factors including imperfect information, contractual restrictions or 'money illusion', a term coined by Keynes to explain the tendency of people to think in nominal rather than real terms. According to classical thinking, if money wages cannot be adjusted downwards to soak up labour supply, the result is unemployment.

The Classicals were also firm supporters of the market mechanism. They believed that market forces, in particular the price mechanism, would, in time, adjust in such a way that would restore the economy back to full employment without the need for government intervention. This, in turn, rested on a belief in Say's Law, after the French economist Jean-Baptiste Say (1767–1832). Say argued that supply creates its own demand. In its simplest form, workers get paid wages for making goods which are then supplied to market. The wages that workers earn for producing goods are then spent on buying the goods that these and other workers have produced. As long as Say's Law continued to operate, the Classicals believed, it would be impossible for high levels of unemployment to persist, and for there to be any involuntary unemployment.

The final element of the classical theory was its take on savings and investment and the relationship that these two variables have with economic growth. The interest rate played the role of equalising the level of savings (income minus consumption) with the level of investment. In other words, the interest rate was able to 'clear' the market for savings (loanable funds) by channelling it into investment, although the interest rate should also be low enough to tempt businesses into borrowing capital. Thus for the Classicals, savings are the main driver of economic growth.

The seeming simplicity of classical theory was harshly exposed by the tumultuous events of the Great Depression, in particular the high level and persistent levels of unemployment that occurred. In such times of turmoil it is common for intellectual rivalries to emerge as competing theories try to capture the high ground by providing coherent explanations of what is occurring. This is precisely what happened in macroeconomics.

The London School of Economics (LSE) had been founded in 1895 by the famous socialists Sydney and Beatrice Webb; the playwright George Bernard Shaw was also a founder member. By 1900 the LSE had established its own Faculty of Economics. Nevertheless, the teaching of economics was still dominated by Marshallian theory and although he had his differences with him, Professor Edwin Cannan, the LSE's most eminent economist in its early days, was still at heart a supporter of Marshall. Consequently, the LSE played second fiddle to Cambridge. However, with Marshall's death in 1924 and Cannan's retirement in 1926, there emerged an opportunity to challenge Cambridge. After the sudden death of Cannan's successor in 1929, the LSE decided to appoint the relatively young Lionel (later Lord) Robbins (1898–1984) to the post of Professor of Political Economy. A large man with Johnsonian looks, Robbins had a reputation as a brilliant lecturer and a fine essayist. Evidence of the latter came in 1932 with the publication of his *An Essay on the Nature and Significance of Economic Science* where Robbins provided what would become the classic definition of economics: 'the science which studies human behaviour as a relationship between ends and scarce means which have alternative uses.'[57]

But despite his charisma and lucid writing, Robbins was not a great theorist and so he was forced to find someone who could match Keynes's theoretical prowess. Helped by his fluency in German, Robbins had developed an interest in Austrian economics, a school founded by Carl Menger (1840–1921) to counterbalance the ideas of the classical economists, Smith and Ricardo in particular. Menger's ideas were picked up by other Austrians, notably Eugen von Böhm-Bawerk, Friedrich von Wieser and Ludwig von Mises (1881–1973). In 1912 Mises had made a name for himself by publishing *The Theory of Money and Credit*, in which he attempted to set out his own theory of money and the business cycle.

Beginning in 1920, Mises had started to run private seminars at the University of Vienna, the aim of which were to discuss, in informal surroundings, the pressing economic issues of the day. Only the very best students were invited to attend, and many of them would later go on to become well known names in their chosen fields, including the co-founder of game theory, Oscar Morgenstern, and Carl Menger's son, the distinguished mathematician, Karl Menger. Another of the attendees was Friedrich von Hayek (1899–1992). Hayek had been born into a modestly aristocratic family in Vienna, his father being a noted botanist. The philosopher Ludwig Wittgenstein was Hayek's second cousin on his mother's

Oscar Morgenstern (1902–77) and the Hungarian mathematical genius John von Neumann (1903–57) were the founders of what is today known as 'game theory'. In *The Theory of Games and Economic Behaviour* (1944) they showed how a situation involving two people, where the behaviour of each person depends on what the other person will do, could be analysed in terms of the different payoffs accruing to each person and what the optimal strategy would be for each person. Interest in game theory has exploded since the 1940s and it now has applications across a variety of disciplines, including biology, computer science and sport.

Friedrich von Hayek (1899–1992), *circa* 1950

side. After serving in the Austrian army in the First World War, Hayek pursued various courses of study at Vienna, before finally being converted to a career in economics after attending the Mises seminars.

Hayek's big break came when he was appointed the first director of the Austrian Institute for Business Cycle Research, which had been set up by Mises in January 1927. It was clear from the beginning that Hayek was a man going places and, becoming increasingly aware of his work, Robbins invited Hayek to deliver a series of lectures at the LSE on monetary theory in 1930–1. With the job situation in Austria rather poor and with the English universities a dominant force in economics, Hayek sensed that the lectures would provide him with an opportunity to not only present his ideas to a new and important audience but also to stake a claim for an appointment at the LSE. His intuition paid off. The lectures were a huge success and were reprinted and published later in 1931 under the title *Prices and Production*. Robbins was convinced that he had found the man to fight Keynes. Hayek was offered and accepted the LSE Tooke Professorship in economics in 1932.

As a man, Hayek was in complete contrast to Keynes. Whereas Keynes was imbued with optimism and a magnetic personality, Hayek was a strange combination of stand-offishness and boldness. He was not helped by his broken English (which allegedly turned into 'hissing'[58] when he got into a muddle whilst lecturing) and often difficult relations with other members of staff. Nicholas (later Lord) Kaldor's relationship with Hayek was particularly telling. Kaldor described how Hayek became 'frightfully annoyed with me. At first he was terribly for me. But then when I discovered he was so silly I sort of teased him, made him look ridiculous, contradicted him in seminars.'[59] It is difficult to imagine Keynes being subject to the same kind of treatment at Cambridge, or anywhere else for that matter, as that dished out by Kaldor to Hayek.

It would be incorrect to assume that the rivalry between Cambridge and London started with Hayek and Keynes; there had been skirmishes before. In 1903 there was an exchange of views in *The Times* between professors from the two universities on the subject of tariff reform[60] while in 1925 Robbins had attacked Keynes's views on monetary policy. There was also, of course, the confrontation between Keynes and Robbins on the Committee of Economists in 1930. The history of economic thought would no doubt have been very different had Keynes accepted an offer to become the LSE's director in 1919; his refusal meant that the post instead went to the social reformer William Beveridge. Nevertheless, it was the debate between Keynes and Hayek in the early 1930s which marked the high point of bilateral tensions.

Hayek's view was that business cycles are caused primarily by over-investment. A change in the money supply causes relative prices to change which, in turn, pushes the market rate of interest below the natural rate (the rate at which supply and demand in the capital market are in equilibrium). As this means that the available return on capital is above the cost of borrowing, firms are more likely to invest in the production of capital goods. Accordingly, production processes become longer. But this production cannot be completed because saving is not large enough to meet the additional demand for borrowing that is required. The result is a downturn. Hayek believed that the only way to alleviate this situation was to let relative prices fall back into equilibrium by themselves, thereby precluding any interventionist role for government. Of course, with the Great Depression in full swing, Hayek's suggestion that governments should sit on their hands did not go down terribly well with policy-makers, not to mention Cambridge.

Much of the controversy between Hayek and Keynes was played out in the pages of the *Economic Journal* and the LSE-based journal

Economica. As the editor of *Economica*, Robbins had asked Hayek to review *A Treatise on Money*, Hayek's comments appearing in two instalments in the August 1931 and February 1932 editions. A taste of Hayek's opinion of the book can be gleaned from the opening page of his first review: '[T]he *Treatise* proves to be so obviously ... the expression of a transitory phase in a process of rapid intellectual development that its appearance cannot be said to have that significance which at one time was expected of it.'[61] Hayek's main point of attack was over Keynes's failure to pay enough attention to the effect that monetary policy supposedly has on the structure of production, a key plank of the Austrian explanation of the cycle.

Keynes was furious. In his private copy of the August 1931 *Economica* he pencilled to himself: *Hayek has not read my book with that measure of 'good will' which an author is entitled to expect of a reader. Until he can do so, he will not see what I mean or know whether I am right. He evidently has a passion which leads him to pick on me, but I am left wondering what this passion is.*[62] Keynes echoed these sentiments in a reply published in *Economica* in November 1931, stating that *Dr. Hayek has seriously misapprehended the character of my conclusions. He thinks that my central contention is something different from what it really is.*[63] Later in the same article, Keynes could not resist a dig at Hayek's *Prices and Production*, claiming that it was *one of the most frightful muddles I have ever read ... It is an extraordinary example of how, starting with a mistake, a remorseless logician can end up in Bedlam.*[64] Private correspondence between Keynes and Hayek lasting from December 1931 to March 1932 failed to make any substantive progress. Still angry over Hayek's review, Keynes asked his Cambridge friend and economist Piero Sraffa (1898–1983) to review *Prices and Production*. Sraffa accepted and was scathing, describing the book as a 'maze of contradictions' which made the reader 'completely dizzy' and 'prepared to believe anything' out of sheer despair.[65] An attempt by Joan Robinson to reconcile Keynes and Hayek with an article in *Economica* in February 1933 failed to have the desired effect.

By the time of *The General Theory*, Hayek had grown tired of controversy and preferred to devote his energies to developing his own ideas. Much to his regret, he never reviewed Keynes's masterpiece, claiming that he believed the book merely contained the latest snapshot of Keynes's views, views which he would quickly ditch before moving on to something else. In this respect, Hayek seriously underestimated the impact of *The General Theory*. Of course, there is no doubting the considerable influence that Hayek's own ideas would have on later generations. His 1944 attack on collectivism in the *Road to Serfdom* quickly became a classic – Keynes for one was an admirer, calling it a *grand book* – even though it took Hayek away from economics and towards political science, whilst his economic theories were revived in the 1970s and 1980s under the monetarist banner championed by right wingers such as Milton Friedman; Hayek's resulting influence on Margaret Thatcher and Ronald Reagan has been well documented. But in the battle of ideas that Hayek had with Keynes in the 1930s, there is no doubt that Hayek came off second best.

With all of the above, one might have expected there to have been rather poor personal relations between Keynes and Hayek. But when the LSE was evacuated to Cambridge during the Second World War, Hayek found himself lodging at King's for a while, where he and Keynes would often share firewatching duties on the College's roof. We can only wonder what conversations they may have had when the time came each evening to change shifts. Keynes also helped Hayek to find a home in Cambridge during the war and supported his election to the British Academy, hardly the actions of a man who held grudges.

Despite his protests at Hayek's critique, Keynes knew that the *Treatise* was defective. There had been some inkling of a change in his thinking before it had even appeared. His falling-out with the Asquiths in 1926 over the General Strike had moved Keynes closer to Lloyd George, a man whom he had parodied only a few years earlier. With the General Election date set for the end of May 1929, Lloyd George was keen to take the Liberals back into the political mainstream and to offer the British people radical new solutions to the high rates of unemployment that they were now faced with. In March 1929 a committee of senior Liberals, including Lloyd George, had published a pamphlet entitled 'We Can Conquer Unemployment!', a call for the government to play a significantly increased role in the economy through various infrastructure schemes, such as an expansion of the public transport network, which would be financed through government borrowing.

The idea of using public works as a means of stimulating economic activity had a long history. Keynes himself had advocated public works as a cure for unemployment in 1924. However, his analysis back then was compromised by the widely held view that the supply of savings and therefore capital was limited: if the government borrowed more from the markets in order to finance public works this would mean that less money would be available to finance investment in the private sector. In what would become known as the 'Treasury view', private investment would be 'crowded out' and the result would be no overall change in employment levels.

With the appearance in May 1929 of *Can Lloyd George Do It?*, a pamphlet Keynes co-authored with Hubert Henderson (then editor of the *Nation and Athenaeum*), the case was again put forward for a public works programme. Keynes had made some headway since 1924 in disposing of the Treasury view, as he now argued that an injection of government investment into the economy would create a *cumulative force of trade activity*,[66] meaning that the knock-on effects of greater state involvement would somehow feed through into greater private sector activity. Unfortunately, there was no way of measuring how strong this 'cumulative force of activity' might be. For example, how many additional jobs would be created if 100 jobs were created through an initial investment by the government? The answer to this question would be contained in a seminal article written by Richard Kahn in 1931. Kahn was one of a small group of brilliant young economists who happened to converge on Cambridge in the late 1920s and early 1930s. With Marshall dead in 1924 and Pigou failing to take the lead that was necessary to push Cambridge economics forward, the group was aware that Keynes, backed by his academic brilliance and personal charisma, was the natural leader amongst the existing faculty. But they had issues with his ideas, in particular the fact that the *Treatise* could not account for high levels of unemployment. So it was that just a few months after the *Treatise* appeared, what would come to be known as the 'Circus' held its first meetings.

Even though membership of the Circus expanded as time went on, it was dominated by a core group of individuals. They were: Richard Kahn, Joan Robinson, James Meade and Piero Sraffa; Joan Robinson's husband Austin was also an important member. The individual relationships that each of these people had with Keynes provides us with some fascinating insights into his and their lives.

Although the other members of the Circus were close associates and even friends of Keynes, there can be little doubt that his closest affinity was with Richard (later Lord) Kahn. The strong intellectual link between Keynes and Kahn began to take shape when Kahn was a 22-year-old economics student at King's: 'Keynes had had good economics students before ... But Richard Ferdinand Kahn was the first who was able and willing to help him in his own work ...'.[67] After securing a First in economics, Kahn then went on to write a highly original fellowship dissertation for King's dealing with the economics of the short run.

Once Kahn's place as Keynes's *favourite pupil* was secured, the two quickly became close friends, Kahn being a frequent visitor to Tilton. Between 1928 and 1946 the two men exchanged no less than 611 letters.[68] Lydia was very fond of Kahn, probably seeing him as a surrogate son, and once stated how proud Maynard would have been on the occasion of Kahn being raised to the peerage in 1965. Kahn also played an active role in managing Lydia's finances after Keynes passed away.

With regard to economics, the contribution that Kahn made to *The General Theory* has been hotly contested. The great Austrian economist Joseph Schumpeter and Roy Harrod took the view that Kahn's role was close to 'co-authorship'. Kahn did act as Keynes's most important bulwark against technical mistakes; indeed, the meticulous nature of Kahn's mind was legendary, a point not lost on Keynes: *I am now engaged in trying to write out ... a really detailed, but nevertheless popular, account of the relation between primary and secondary employment. I hope I don't make any bloomers, – I wish you were here to look over my shoulder.*[69] Kahn himself was of the opinion that his input was indeed an important one but that it was more in a supporting role than anything else.

Joan Robinson was the second key member of the Circus. Joan Maurice, as she was before she married, had gone up to Cambridge in 1922 to study economics as an undergraduate at the all-female Girton College. Much to her disappointment, she only managed an Upper Second Class degree. Nevertheless, it was clear that Maurice had a talent for the subject. After marrying fellow Cambridge economist Austin Robinson, she secured an assistant lectureship in the Economics Faculty in 1931. Later on in the 1930s, she would become increasingly interested in Marxist economics, while remaining one of Keynes's greatest disciples, writing an *Introduction to the Theory of Employment* in 1937, a 'told to the children' version of Keynes's ideas, as well as extending *The General Theory* to the open economy and the Marshallian long run.

She was without doubt the most important female economist ever to have lived, although her great contributions were sadly never recognised by the awarding of a Nobel Prize.

Although Robinson allegedly feared only Sraffa when it came to debating matters of economics, she clearly held Keynes in great respect. In return, Keynes viewed Robinson as integral to his own intellectual endeavours. Keynes would often seek out her opinion when he was having difficulties trying to convince other economists of his views, and was happy for her to be privy to various draft versions of *The General Theory*: *Here is a first instalment, namely Book I. The rest will follow shortly. Chapters 1 to 6 and 20–25 are in a more advanced stage of revision than the intervening chapters. I shall be extremely grateful for any criticisms, of form or substance.*[70] In turn, Robinson was very close to Kahn. As he had done with Keynes, Kahn provided extensive advice and guidance to Robinson as she developed what would turn out to be her highly influential theory of imperfect competition. The two became close on a personal level and an affair ensued.

After completing his undergraduate studies at Oxford, James Meade (1907–95) had gone to Cambridge to pursue postgraduate work. At the time of the Circus's meetings he was just 23, the youngest member of the core group. Meade's role has arguably been overlooked by historians, who have preferred to concentrate on Kahn and Robinson. However, as Austin Robinson has claimed, Meade was 'more active than any of us',[71] not least perhaps because of the amount of spare time that he had at his disposal as a result of his student status. Nevertheless, given that Meade was so young, coupled with the fact that the other members of the Circus were already well on their way to becoming eminent economists in their own right, his contribution, which was often technically sophisticated, becomes even more impressive. Even Keynes, who was rarely stumped when it came to technical matters, was puzzled and 'looked around the room for "Mr Meade's Relation" on first acquaintance'.[72] On the back of Kahn's formalisation of the so-called 'multiplier' process, which we shall come to shortly, Meade had shown how the extra income created by an increase in investment would, in turn, create a level of additional savings that would be equal to the original injection of investment.

Keynes considered Meade to be of considerable promise, whilst Meade considered Keynes to be 'God'. As far as Keynesian economics was concerned, Meade would later claim that he had the basic elements of what was to become *The General Theory* in his head when he returned to Oxford in the autumn of 1931. Although this was probably an exaggeration, Meade was a lifelong advocate of Keynes's ideas, his support playing a crucial role in shaping British economic policy after the Second World War. Interestingly, of the main Circus members, Meade was the only one to receive the Nobel Prize for Economics.

The last prominent member of the Circus was Piero Sraffa. In early 1931 he was also the oldest, aged 32. After having offended Mussolini's Fascist government, Sraffa managed to escape to Cambridge in 1927 and soon became a close friend of Ludwig Wittgenstein (on whose philosophical development Sraffa had a great influence) and Keynes. Socially, Keynes and Sraffa could often be found visiting Cambridge's various antiquarian bookshops of a Saturday afternoon, on the lookout for a bargain; Keynes fondly referred to this as *pottering with Piero*. One of the more curious aspects of Sraffa's personality was his horror of speaking in front of large audiences. Indeed, it was not unknown for him to become physically sick just before he was due to deliver a lecture, the result being that it either had to be postponed or a stand-in had to be found. Luckily for Sraffa, Keynes was sympathetic to such eccentricities and was instrumental in finding Sraffa a series of jobs in order to keep him in Cambridge. This included editing the Royal Economic Society's edition of Ricardo's *Works and Correspondence*.

Sraffa started work on the project in 1930. The first of 11 volumes did not appear until 1951 and it would be a further 22 years before the final edition appeared, testament to another of Sraffa's horrors, that of publishing.

Even before his escape from Italy, Sraffa was familiar with Keynes's work, having translated *A Tract on Monetary Reform* into Italian in 1925. Despite this, the two men had decidedly different views on economics. Keynes found Sraffa's preoccupation with Marx and Ricardo rather odd whilst Sraffa, despite being a member of the Circus, did not agree with many of the ideas that would eventually appear in *The General Theory*, in particular Keynes's theory of liquidity preference. Joan Robinson was aware of Sraffa's apathy towards the new economics, claiming that he 'never really quite knew what it was that we [Keynes and the Circus] were going on about.'[73]

Although the individual members of the Circus continued in their own way to influence Keynes in subsequent years, it was in the relatively short period between January and May 1931 that the intellectual buzz surrounding the group was at its height. Initially, their relatively informal talks took place in Kahn's rooms at King's but were later expanded to more formal discussions at Trinity College; Kahn acted as the go-between, or 'Messenger Angel' as he became affectionately known, relaying messages from the Circus to Keynes and vice versa. Potential attendees at the Circus were put through a rigorous qualifying interview by Kahn and other senior members. Keynes chose not to attend, concerned that his sheer presence would probably have been overawing. The inability of most people to keep up with the speed of his mind could also have compromised the Circus's discussions. Other non-attendees included the reclusive Pigou and Dennis Robertson, another Cambridge economics don whose *Banking Policy and the Price Level* (1926) made a strong impression on Keynes. Sadly, Robertson and Keynes would later fall out over Robertson's rejection of Keynesianism.

Unfortunately, the Circus never kept a formal record of its discussions. This makes any attempted reconstruction of what may have been said extremely difficult. Luckily, the collective subsequent recollections of the Circus's members give some clues to its role. Undoubtedly the most important contribution was its success in convincing Keynes of the need to change the main plank of his analysis away from a focus on prices and towards changes in output. The predominance of the quantity theory had meant that ever since he had first started to study economics, Keynes had been shackled to the notion that it was changes in prices that were the key factor in explaining business cycles. According to this view, it was very difficult to use economic policy to stimulate changes in output. In other words, output was treated as if it were fixed.

In *Can Lloyd George Do It?* Keynes had hinted that the fixed output assumption might be wrong and that if the government could control changes in output through adjustments in investment and fiscal policy then the resulting *cumulative force of activity* might be a way of pulling the economy out of recession or depression. The Circus persuaded Keynes that output was not necessarily a given. During an economic upturn for example it was quite reasonable to expect that producers might respond to increased consumption by raising output rather than by raising prices. The Circus also helped Keynes to clarify a number of other issues, such as making more precise his definitions of important economic variables and clarifying the use of accounting identities.[74]

However, Keynes still had to provide a convincing rebuttal of the Treasury view that an increase in government investment would simply divert funds away from the private sector. In such circumstances, it would be difficult to support a programme of public works, i.e. a fiscal injection. The key lay in Keynes's phrase the *cumulative force of activity* from *Can Lloyd George Do It?*. If a way could be found to formalise this idea, the Treasury view would be debunked. The breakthrough came in June 1931 with the publication in the *Economic Journal* of an article by Kahn entitled 'The Relation of Home Investment to Unemployment'. What Kahn did was mathematically model the various effects an increase in government spending would have on the economy. He showed how the initial spending would be spent in successive rounds and how this would lead to increased employment. Kahn also demonstrated that there would be various 'leakages', including savings and spending on imports, which would eventually limit the 'multiplier' effects of the initial spending.

The Circus and Kahn's multiplier in particular certainly played an important role in helping to point the way to *The General Theory*. It is also worth remembering that Keynes's attitude towards what his younger colleagues were up to was broadly welcoming. For a man who had just spent six years writing a treatise (more or less in isolation) which any other economist would have been happy to consider as the *pièce de résistance* of their life's work and who continued to also be deeply involved in official work, one might have expected a less-than-positive response from Keynes on hearing the news that a group of juniors had decided to discuss every last detail of his latest thinking. But as was typical of the man, Keynes saw the Circus as an opportunity and 'picked up [its] ideas, sometimes only after extensive discussion, incorporated them into his own thinking and went ahead.'[75] There is even some evidence to suggest that the Circus may at one point have been ahead of Keynes, although this did not last very long and the initiative always resided with Keynes.

By the beginning of the 1932 academic year, changes in Keynes's thinking began to show themselves in the lectures he delivered to Cambridge undergraduates. Thus in autumn 1932, Keynes's previous lecture entitled 'The Pure Theory of Money', reflecting the influence of the *Treatise*, had become 'The Monetary Theory of Production'.[76] Meanwhile, in October of that year, a group of Cambridge economists, including Keynes and Pigou, wrote to *The Times* in support of the case for increased public expenditure as a means of alleviating and possibly curing the downturn. With Hayek's aversion to any role being played by the government in attempting to boost economic activity, it was no surprise that a group of LSE economists, headed by Hayek and Robbins, also wrote to *The Times* opposing increased state spending.

Undeterred, Keynes ploughed on. In March 1933, he penned a further four articles for *The Times*, under the heading 'The Means to Prosperity' and in April published 'The Multiplier' in the *New Statesman and Nation*. Although it no longer held formal meetings, Circus members continued to 'spy' on Keynes's progress by attending, and subsequently commenting on, his lectures whilst he would return the favour by regularly sounding out Kahn and Robinson for their opinions on his latest drafts of *The General Theory*. Even in the early months of 1934, Keynes was still highly appreciative of Kahn's help, commenting to Robinson that, *I am going through a stiff week's supervision from R.F.K. {Kahn} on my M.S. He is a marvellous critic and suggester and improver – there never was anyone in the history of the world to whom it was so helpful to submit one's stuff.*[77]

Although Keynes was no longer directly involved in government work and his commitments at Cambridge had become less, work on *The General Theory* continued to be interrupted. Keynes was still a very active investor and was involved in various companies. However, his contributions as an economist were beginning to be formally recognised by academia with Columbia University in the US granting him an honorary doctorate in the spring of 1934. During his trip, Keynes took the opportunity to pop in for an hour-long chat with President Roosevelt, the President reporting that he had 'a grand talk with K and liked him immensely'.[78] Keynes, once again indulging his fixation with people's hands, was

President Franklin D Roosevelt in 1933

less complimentary: *Rather disappointing. Firm and fairly strong, but not clever or with finesse, shortish round nails like those at the end of a business-man's fingers.*[79]

Meanwhile, the main elements of *The General Theory* were in place by the time Keynes returned to Britain. On the first day of 1935, he was able to confidently write to his old friend George Bernard Shaw: *To understand my state of mind ... you have to know that I believe myself to be writing a book on economic theory which will largely revolutionise – not, I suppose, at once but in the course of the next ten years – the way the world thinks about economic problems … I can't expect you, or anyone else, to believe this at the present stage. But for myself I don't merely hope what I say, in my own mind I'm quite sure.*[80]

It would be another year before Keynes's 'revolutionary' book hit the shelves.

A significant chunk of Keynes's time in 1935 was taken up by the financing and construction of the Arts Theatre in Cambridge. The original cost of construction had been put at £18,000, Keynes stumping up a significant proportion of this. As with many building projects, the costs of construction soared as the theatre was made bigger and a restaurant was added. By the time of its completion, it had swallowed up £36,000.[81] Keynes was involved in every last detail of the theatre's running, right up to the opening night on 3 February 1936, when it hosted a production by the Vic-Wells Ballet. Shortly after, Lydia performed at the theatre to rave reviews. As a gesture of goodwill, Keynes gave the theatre to the City of Cambridge in 1938 and it continues to operate successfully to this day.

Not many people, let alone economists, can have experienced the exhilaration that Maynard Keynes must have felt on the two days of 3 and 4 February 1936: on the evening of the 3rd he had realised his personal vision of providing a new centre of high culture for Cambridge whilst just a few hours later, on the morning of the 4th, his masterpiece and one of the most influential books ever to have been written, *The General Theory of Employment, Interest and Money*, was published. As with nearly all his books, Keynes had arranged for Macmillan to be the publisher. Keynes would meet all production and advertising costs while Macmillan would receive a commission on costs. This meant that *The General Theory* was priced at just 5 shillings, deliberately cheap in order to encourage readership amongst undergraduates, but a signal that the book was an important one which deserved to be read and absorbed.

Keynes was not wrong in this last respect. Before its release, there had been rumblings about what it might contain. Insights into Keynes's thinking had already appeared in other places. But when the book was actually published, many academic economists, let alone undergraduates in the subject, had trouble understanding what Keynes was trying to get at. Part of the problem lay in the fact that it was badly organised and was not characterised by Keynes's usual flair with the written word. Nevertheless, there was no doubting its brilliance. Paul Samuelson, himself one of the great economists of the 20th century and a firm Keynesian, summed up his view of *The General Theory* thus: 'It is a badly written book, poorly organised; any layman who, beguiled by the author's previous reputation, bought the book was cheated of his 5 shillings. It is not well suited for classroom use. It is arrogant, bad-tempered, polemical, and not overly-generous in its acknowledgements. It abounds in mares' nests and confusions ... In it the Keynesian system stands out indistinctly ... Flashes of insight and intuition intersperse tedious algebra. An awkward definition suddenly gives way to an unforgettable cadenza. When it finally is mastered, we find its analysis to be obvious and at the same time new. In short, it is a work of genius.'[82] The fact that the book was badly organised was indeed surprising giving how long it took to write, how many drafts it went through and how many talented people were privy to its drafts. There was even speculation that Keynes did not fully understand his own theory!

The General Theory is certainly wide-ranging, covering topics including the 'principal of effective [i.e. aggregate] demand', the 'marginal efficiency of capital', the 'psychological and business incentives to liquidity', the 'essential properties of interest and money', and the 'theory of prices'. Bringing these various strands together in order to produce a coherent whole was always going to be difficult and it is perhaps not surprising that ambiguities arose. Keynes was also a man trying to escape from the theories that had been drilled into him ever since he had picked up Marshall's *Principles* back in 1905. In a memorable passage, Keynes described this as a *long struggle of escape ... a struggle of escape from habitual modes of thought and expression. The ideas which are here expressed so laboriously are extremely simple and should be obvious. The difficulty lies, not in the new ideas, but in escaping from the old ones, which ramify, for those brought up as most of us have been, into every corner of our minds.*[83]

In the preface, Keynes tried to provide a brief outline of his theory, all the time focusing on the fundamental idea that the fixed output assumption was wrong: *When I finished {A Treatise on Money}, I had made some progress towards pushing monetary theory back to becoming a theory of output as a whole. But my lack of emancipation from preconceived ideas showed itself in what now seems to me to be the outstanding fault of the theoretical parts of that work ... that I failed to deal thoroughly with the effects of changes in the level of output. My so-called 'fundamental equations' were an instantaneous picture taken on the assumption of a given output ... This book, on the other hand, has evolved into what is primarily a study of the forces which determine changes in the scale of output and employment as a whole ...*[84]

In a reversal of Say's Law, Keynes proceeded to show the primacy of effective demand rather than supply in determining the course of the business cycle. Keynes's view was that the investment activity of firms is determined by the consumption behaviour of individuals, not their savings behaviour. In other words, if savings are greater than investment at full employment because, say, of previous over-investment, there will be a deterioration in firms' *animal spirits* which manifests itself in the form of lower investment in capital and labour. In the latter case, this leads to increased unemployment; Keynes referred to this situation as the 'Paradox of Thrift'. Moreover, aggregate demand and aggregate supply may be in equilibrium but this could be at a level below full employment.

In contrast to the Classicals, Keynes agreed that the interest rate depended instead on the supply and demand for money, variables that could not adjust quickly enough to clear an excess of saving, thus blunting the effectiveness of monetary policy. Keynes also cast doubt on the efficacy of adjusting money wages as a means of aiding recovery, arguing that it was a relatively inexact measure and would probably take too long to have any effect due to the presence of wage stickiness. Even if money wages are very flexible, Keynes argued, any rapid downward movement could be disastrous as it might set off a deflationary spiral.

Keynes's answer to the above was that investment and consumption had to be stimulated at the expense of savings. The only economic agent with the power to achieve this was the State. In the confusion that ensued over 'Keynesian economics and the economics of Keynes' – driven partly, it has to be said, by the ambiguity of *The General Theory* itself – so-called 'functional finance' became intimately associated with Keynes's name. Keynes never specifically came out in favour of governments running budget deficits, either through the lowering of taxes or increased public expenditure, as a means of boosting the economy. What Keynes actually supported was a 'socialisation of investment', whereby the government would take a greater part in determining the distribution and size of investment activity. The multiplier would ensure that the positive effect that an initial investment has on employment and incomes would be repeated through successive rounds of spending, with the magnitude of this additional spending depending on consumers' 'marginal propensity to consume', i.e. how much of an extra £1 of income they spent rather than saved. Keynes himself was conscious of how his ideas might be interpreted beyond the meaning he had intended for them. Once, after dining with what were supposed to be a group of like-minded American economists, he quipped that he had been the only non-Keynesian at the table!

What was new about *The General Theory*? It certainly contained a number of innovations, such as an emphasis on the short run, a focus on psychological factors (including animal spirits and uncertainty), and Keynes's argument that classical theory should be considered as a special case, relevant only in conditions of full employment, whilst his own 'general' theory applied in all other circumstances. At the same time, Keynes did utilise a number of pre-existing theories. For example, the principle of effective demand had been around since Malthus's time in the late 18th century and the notion that under-consumption could be responsible for the cycle had also been proposed before. Nevertheless, *The General Theory* was the first attempt to bring together all of these existing ideas on business cycle theory, Keynes then synthesising them with his own insights. In this sense, *The General Theory* was a truly revolutionary work.

Keynes ended *The General Theory* on a philosophical note. In what has probably become the most recognised passage from all his works and in an echo of the words he had penned to George Bernard Shaw at the beginning of 1935, Keynes indicated just how aware he was of the impact *The General Theory* was likely to make in the years ahead: *{T}he ideas of economists and political philosophers, both when they are right and when they are wrong, are more powerful than is commonly understood. Indeed the world is ruled by little else. Practical men, who believe themselves to be quite exempt from any intellectual influences, are usually the slaves of some defunct economist. Madmen in authority, who hear voices in the air, are distilling their frenzy from some academic scribbler of a few years back. I am sure that the power of vested interests is vastly exaggerated compared with the gradual encroachment of ideas. Not, indeed, immediately, but after a certain interval; for in the field of economic and political philosophy there are not many who are influenced by new theories after they are twenty-five* *or thirty years of age, so that the ideas which civil servants and politicians and even agitators apply to current events are not likely to be the newest. But, soon or late, it is ideas, not vested interests, which are dangerous for good or evil.*[85]

Aftermath of *The General Theory* 1936–9

With *The General Theory* set loose upon the world, Keynes had produced his masterpiece, the tract that he had been pursuing all his adult life, the *tour de force* that would place him in the pantheon of the great economists. There was nevertheless the small matter of everyday life to be getting on with. For most people, making the adjustment would be a difficult one. But Keynes seemed to have the ability to rapidly change his focus of attention when required, whatever the situation. His mind was constantly alert to where he could make a difference or be of some help. Even if it was at the mundane level of improving the food at the Arts Theatre, Keynes felt obliged to get involved.

He was also a man of routine, at least as far as his movements between Cambridge, London and Tilton were concerned (although his poor state of health often disrupted his travel plans). From just after the First World War right up until 1937, he would spend term time in Cambridge from Thursday evening through the weekend, before leaving for London on Tuesday afternoon. Keynes still had strong links with Cambridge, despite the fact that he was no longer attached to the Economics Faculty after resigning his lectureship in 1920. Indeed, his only purely academic connection with the University was his Fellowship at King's.

Notwithstanding all of this, Keynes had a dominant presence at Cambridge. He continued to supervise undergraduates, ran the financial affairs of King's in his role as First Bursar and attended gatherings of the Political Economy Club. Every Sunday morning he would meet Austin Robinson to decide what should be included in the next edition of the *Economic Journal* and in the afternoon he would often spend time with his parents at Harvey Road. On Wednesdays, Keynes was in London where he would fulfil his commitments as chairman of the National Mutual Life Assurance Company and socialise with his network of London friends. During the Cambridge vacations, he could usually be found either in London or Tilton. There was also time to deliver a radio broadcast for the BBC in August 1936 on a subject close to Keynes's heart: Art and the State.[86]

Meanwhile, *The General Theory* hovered in the background. Keynes would no doubt have been happy to let the world get on with debating his book whilst he stood on the sidelines looking on wryly, thinking up his next blockbuster. Indeed, he was surprisingly standoffish (although not exclusively so) when it came to defending the book's claims. The Bloomsbury Group would have approved, but it was not in Keynes's nature to let matters pass completely, especially as *The General Theory* had attracted so much attention, both from supporters and detractors.

One of the earliest semi-public discussions that Keynes was personally involved in took place on 2 May 1936 when Hubert Henderson, who had jointly authored *Can Lloyd George Do It?* with Keynes, was invited by the undergraduate Marshall Society at Cambridge to discuss *The General Theory*. Given Henderson's previous working relationship with Keynes, a sympathetic treatment might have been expected. Surprisingly, however, Henderson was rather critical, although as Keynes noted in a letter to Lydia, there was little substance to his arguments. Moreover, Keynes delighted in the loyalty to *The General Theory* displayed by Kahn and Robinson at the meeting: *I was astonished at the violence of his {Henderson's} emotion against it {The General Theory}:*

he thinks it a poisonous book; yet when it came to the debate there was very little of the argument which he was really prepared to oppose. He came off badly in the debate with Joan and Alexander [Keynes's nickname for Kahn] *and myself barking round him. The undergraduates enjoyed the cockfight outrageously. One got the impression that he was not really much interested in pure economic theory, but much disliked for emotional or political reasons some of the practical conclusions to which my arguments seemed to point. As a theoretical attack there was almost nothing to answer.*[87]

Outside Cambridge, discussion of *The General Theory* was being carried on furiously. As a measure of the level of interest in the book, over 125 English-language reviews had appeared by the end of 1936.[88] Their tone and content was varied, to say the least. At the more extreme end was an article entitled 'What Does Mr Keynes Want – Poison Gas?', written by one Henry Douglas and published by the British newspaper, the *Morning Star*, well known for its communist leanings. Douglas attacked Keynes for not discussing Marxist theories and for producing a theory which allegedly supported British imperialism. Many reviewers simply didn't understand what *The General Theory* was trying to say and pleaded for it to be 'translated'. Others were bemused by Keynes's suggestion that unemployment could be alleviated by employing men to dig up bottles of buried money!

Of course, there were more serious assessments. One was

Karl Marx (1818–83), German philosopher and economist. With Friedrich Engels, he wrote *The Communist Manifesto* in 1848, which laid the basis of communism. This was followed in 1867 by the first volume of *Das Kapital*. Marx employed the dialectical method of Hegel to argue that fundamental changes in the way society operates are brought about through conflict and that economic forces would eventually lead to the collapse of the capitalist system to be replaced by communism. Keynes never took to Marx, describing *Das Kapital* as *out-of-date, academic controversialising.*

by Keynes's old teacher at Cambridge, A C Pigou. Pigou had been asked to review *The General Theory* for *Economica*, this after nobody could be found at the LSE to take on the task. Pigou was critical of Keynes, unsurprising as Keynes had taken Pigou's *The Theory of Unemployment* (1933) as the most fully developed exposition of Classical economics, an exposition which Keynes then proceeded to demolish. Pigou was particularly scathing about Keynes's tendency to mock his opponents, a habit he picked up from Bloomsbury. Pigou responded in kind, stating that 'Einstein actually did for Physics what Mr. Keynes believes himself to have done for Economics. He developed a far-reaching generalisation, under which Newton's results can be subsumed as a special case. But he [Einstein] did not, in announcing his discovery, insinuate, through carefully barbed sentences, that Newton and those who had hitherto followed his lead were a gang of incompetent bunglers.'[89] Long after Keynes's death, however, even Pigou would recant and acknowledge the importance of *The General Theory*.

Meanwhile, in the US the reviewers were generally more hostile than their British counterparts, although there was some easing in opinion as time went on. Representative of this were two pieces by Alvin Hansen, then a professor of economics at the University of Minnesota and soon to be a professor at Harvard where he would become Keynes's greatest American disciple. In his first review written for the June 1936 edition of the *Yale Review*, Hansen was critical of *The General Theory*'s assumption of a rigid economy. Hansen argued that, 'It is reasonably safe to predict that Keynes's new book will, so far as his theoretical apparatus is concerned, fare little better than did the "Treatise."'[90] However, after just a few months of reflection, Hansen had (unaccountably) become more sympathetic, stating that 'Keynes's new book, as with everything which comes from his pen, will stimulate thinking on fresh lines in the field of economic dynamics.'[91] He still accused Keynes of using unconvincing arguments and suggested that the '[*General Theory*] is more a symptom of economic trends than a foundation stone upon which a science can be built'.[92] Nevertheless, it was clear that Hansen was becoming a convert.

At this point, it is probably worth asking why exactly *The General Theory* succeeded in making a major impact. To begin with, there was the fairly obvious point that it came along at the right time, providing as it did a coherent attempt at explaining what had happened during the Great Depression and what could be done to avoid such situations in the future. This 'policy relevance' argument had played a major part in the downfall of Hayek's 'do nothing' approach to economic crises, allowing Keynes to step into the breach. After the war, *The General Theory* would provide politicians and civil servants with the justification they needed to implement Keynesian-inspired economic policies. This in turn helped to create the 'Golden Age' of strong economic growth and low inflation for many of the world's developed nations from 1950 to 1973 and the so-called 'Military Keynesianism' of the 1980s pursued by the Reagan administration which combined tax cuts with a substantial expansion in spending on the military. A further sense in which *The General Theory* came along at the right time was that it didn't have to contend with potential criticism from some of the heavyweights who had dominated the economics profession in Keynes's childhood. Many of these individuals had died in the 1920s, including Marshall, of course, but also Edgeworth and Menger. With what has been dubbed the 'Years of High Theory' starting in 1926, '[a] fresh start could be made without these giants peering over men's shoulders'.[93]

A final reason for Keynes's success was that he already had a reputation as a man willing to challenge convention. There was indeed a great sense of anticipation in the period leading up to *The General Theory*'s appearance and not only in Britain. In the US, Paul Samuelson likened the arrival at Harvard of the first copies of *The General Theory* – the undergraduates had put in a special order to ensure that the book reached them as quickly as possible – to the great emotion that Keats experienced as retold in his *On First Looking into Chapman's Homer*.[94] Keynes was also, of course, an extremely competent theorist. Without *A Tract on Monetary Reform* and *A Treatise on Money* behind him, it would have been entirely possible 'that if the *General Theory* had been his [Keynes's] first publication, it would probably have been dismissed as the work of a clever but pretentious crank. Recognition would certainly have been much slower'.[95] In other words, Keynes benefited from what sociologists refer to as the 'Matthew Effect'. Inspired by the New Testament, this broadly means that the rich get richer and the poor get poorer. In Keynes's case, his new idea that the economy could be in equilibrium below full employment had a much greater chance of succeeding than if it had been proposed by someone without an established reputation. On the back of this, Keynes's claim to have discovered a 'general' theory of economics became more believable.

In the early days after *The General Theory*'s appearance, Keynes was happy to personally push his new theory onto the world, as a trip to Sweden in September 1936 to deliver a stout defence of his ideas showed. Later in the year, in what turned out to be his only major published response to his critics, Keynes penned an article for the *Quarterly Journal of Economics* (it actually appeared in the February 1937 edition) in which he commented on a series of four separate articles on *The General Theory*, including one by the hostile Dennis Robertson. Keynes attempted again to set out his theory, this time with a greater emphasis on the role played by uncertainty in the business cycle, arguing that *we have, as a rule, only the vaguest idea of any but the most direct consequences of our acts*.[96] Keynes also had plans to write some footnotes to *The General Theory*. Sadly, a deterioration in his health in 1937 precluded this, an unfortunate episode in the history of ideas as a follow-up to *The*

General Theory would undoubtedly have helped to eliminate much of the subsequent confusion over what Keynes actually meant.

Since childhood, Keynes had suffered various ailments. Although *The General Theory* was now complete, the many years of toil had taken a tremendous toll on his health. He was still only in his early fifties. Matters started coming to a head in late 1936 and early 1937 when he suffered a serious bout of influenza. There was a minor recovery, before he reported to Lydia in late January that *My breathing muscles were so wonky to-day that I only just managed to walk to Harvey Rd ... The complaint is exactly what I thought it was – rheumatism in the little muscles of the chest* plus *post-influenza*.[97] Keynes carried on working, a series of three articles on 'How to Avoid a Slump' appearing in *The Times* in mid-January where for the first time he attempted to apply *The General Theory* to prevailing economic conditions. But his health got no better. In March he was examined by Sir Walter Langdon-Brown, his mother's brother and a well-known doctor of his day. An X-ray of Keynes's chest revealed that his heart had been damaged by the bout of influenza and by his smoking (although this wouldn't have been realised at the time). Langdon-Brown recommended a period of rest and a heart tonic. Frustrated by his condition, Keynes complained over the Easter vacation that he had *to behave as though {he} were feeble*.[98]

By early May he was still in a bad way and on 16 May suffered a major heart attack. His life hung in the balance. He was ordered to stay in bed at Harvey Road for a prolonged period, under the care of Lydia and Florence. He remained in Cambridge for a month, by which point his health had recovered sufficiently enough for him to be moved for convalescence at Ruthin Castle in North Wales, well away from the pressures of academic and professional life. However, even at Ruthin his mind worked incessantly, despite the fact that his body had failed. Forever watchful, Lydia moved into a hotel next door to the castle, although this didn't prevent Keynes sneaking out the odd letter, including one to the Chancellor of the Exchequer.

By September, the doctors were satisfied that Keynes's condition had improved to the point where he could be released. He returned to Tilton at the end of the month, still under orders not to exert himself, either physically or mentally. There was some slackening, with Keynes relying increasingly on Kahn to assist in the running of King's finances and on Austin Robinson to oversee the publication of the *Economic Journal*. Keynes, meanwhile, turned his attentions to matters closer to home and the running of the 300 acres of farmland (including a piggery) at Tilton. He had always fancied himself as something of a country squire and his acquisition of a 50-year lease on Tilton in 1936 turned this into reality. After Keynes's death, the farm manager at Tilton, Logan Thomson, who lived just across the way, would play an increasingly important part in looking after Lydia's affairs, the two of them forming a close friendship in the process.

By Christmas 1937, Keynes was still fragile, Lydia playing the role of the protective nurse. A marked deterioration in Keynes's financial position as a result of a stock market downturn didn't help. There was some return to normality at Tilton with Duncan and Vanessa walking over from Charleston and Leonard and Virginia Woolf making the short trip from Rodmell. A recovery in the early months of 1938 enabled Keynes to make his first public appearance on 23 February to give his annual speech as chairman of the National Mutual. However, it turned out to be his last as the board, unhappy about the losses the company had suffered in the 1937 downturn on the back of Keynes's investment advice, forced him to resign. But there were plenty of other things to keep him busy, such as meetings of the Council of the Royal Economic Society which were now held at his London home in Gordon Square.

With Keynes's health so delicate, much of the task of trying to spread the Keynesian gospel now had to be left to other people. Keynes himself was acutely aware of the importance of disciples in helping to get his message across. Although Kahn and Robinson had already demonstrated their very vocal support, Keynes still felt isolated. Writing to Roy Harrod, who would become perhaps his greatest champion in Britain, Keynes complained in August 1936 how *experience seems to show that people are divided between the old ones whom nothing will shift and are merely amazed by my attempts to underline the points of transition so vital in my own progress, and the young ones who have not been properly brought up and believe nothing in particular ... I have no companions it seems, in my own generation, either of earliest teachers or of earliest pupils.*[99]

Sir Roy Harrod (1900–78) was educated at Westminster and New College, Oxford. Keynes regarded Harrod highly whilst Harrod held a deep affection for Keynes. Harrod wrote the full first-length biography of Keynes which, although competently written, glossed over various aspects of Keynes's life, in particular his homosexuality. During the Second World War, Harrod would serve in 'S' branch, a role that brought him into regular contact with Churchill.

Keynes was being overly pessimistic. Although he may have had trouble convincing his contemporaries of the validity of his ideas, there were a number of younger economists who were willing to step up to the plate. A 'Keynesian School' quickly flourished. As noted, a key disciple in Britain was Sir Roy Harrod. Harrod was an economist at the University of Oxford from the 1920s to the 1960s, who spent the autumn of 1922 at Cambridge studying economics under Keynes. Through their extensive correspondence, Harrod had a significant influence on Keynes during the writing of *The General Theory*. The fact that Harrod became such an important defender of Keynes was probably at least partly down to the influence of Kahn who wrote to Harrod as early as 1934 that he was 'one of the few economists in the whole world on whom Maynard can reckon. I do not add the words "outside Cambridge" because the number of Cambridge economists who can really be regarded as Maynard's supporters is a vanishingly small quantity. Such as we are, we do very much look to you as a leader in what must after all be described as a fight.'[100] Harrod would later go on to develop, amongst other things, the concept of a 'warranted rate of growth', which attempted to extend the Keynesian system by identifying the rate of economic growth at which all savings are continually absorbed as investment.

The Keynesian avalanche rapidly gathered pace and was in full swing by the end of the decade. Hayek and the LSE were certainly overwhelmed. Indeed, one of the symptoms of Keynes's growing ascendancy was the switch in loyalties away from Hayek and towards Keynes that took place amongst LSE students and staff as the 1930s progressed. For example, Nicholas Kaldor's switch was confirmed by a distinctly Keynesian article on wages and unemployment article in the 1937 *Economic Journal*. After this, Kaldor was increasingly drawn to the Keynesians, spending much of the Second World War at Cambridge before becoming a fellow at King's in 1949 and a professor of economics at the University in 1965.

Just as interesting was the case of Abba Lerner (1903–82). Before entering the LSE in 1929, Lerner had been a machinist, a teacher and had also dabbled in business. After completing his undergraduate studies, he took up a lectureship at the LSE, a post he held from 1930 to 1937. During this time he spent six months at Cambridge in 1934–5 where he came into contact with Keynes and where the seeds of his interest in Keynes's ideas were sown. By 1936, Lerner had become a full convert, in the process rejecting

Hayek. His conversion to Keynesianism was made final in June 1936 when he wrote a sympathetic review of *The General Theory*, sending a copy of it to Keynes. Keynes was more than grateful for the support, writing to Lerner that *I think your article is splendid. You have succeeded in getting a most accurate and convincing story into a small space ... I am extremely grateful to you for having been at so much pains to explain matters. From the news which reaches me, I am sure you have been remarkably successful.*[101]

In the 1930s Lerner was also one of the attendees at regular meetings, held half way between Cambridge and London at Bishop's Stortford, where the Cambridge economists would try to explain to their LSE colleagues the Keynesian message in an attempt to win them over. Although Keynes never attended these gatherings, they were led by no less a figure than Joan Robinson. In what must have been a fascinating series of discussions, Lerner describes how the two tribes once met for a whole weekend. The meeting was not wholly successful. Nevertheless, it was one of London's first introductions to Keynesianism by one of its leading architects and advocates: '[It] was Joan Robinson in charge, and as we would try to understand, she'd say, "Yes, that's right; now you're getting the idea ... No, no; now you've gone backwards." When the weekend was over we still didn't know what they were talking about ... They were confident that we were either just very stupid or backward – and we thought they were crazy, obviously doing something that didn't make sense, but we couldn't quite put our finger on what was wrong.'[102] Nevertheless, over subsequent years, Lerner's appreciation of Keynesianism grew considerably to the point where in 1944 he published what came to be the highly influential theory of 'fine-tuning' or 'functional finance', the basic message of which was that governments should not always try to balance their budgets but rather should be more concerned with using budget deficits and surpluses as a means of controlling the economy.

Meanwhile, the Oxford-educated John Hicks (1904–89) was also at the LSE in the early 1930s, having secured a temporary lectureship in economics. At the relatively tender age of 30, it was clear that Hicks was destined to become one of the greats, co-authoring one of *the* seminal papers on the theory of value in 1934. Keynes had become aware of Hicks's work a couple of years earlier when Macmillan had asked him for his opinion of a manuscript Hicks had sent them entitled *The Theory of Wages*. Although it would become a standard work in its field, in Keynes's opinion it was a *highly theoretical book, the serious and careful work of an unoriginal but competent mind*.[103]

Back at the LSE, any lingering hope that Hayek may have had of Hicks coming to his support in the battle with Cambridge vanished when Hicks left in 1935 to take up a lectureship at Cambridge on the invitation of Pigou. He was too late to take on a significant role in the group around Keynes, but made up for it in 1937 by the publication of what is probably the best known formal model in economics, the 'IS/LM', a diagrammatic representation of *The General Theory* showing the relationship between investment and savings on the one hand and liquidity preference and money supply on the other. Keynes found IS/LM interesting and had no major criticism of it, although both Kahn and Robinson objected to what they saw as its over-simplification of *The General Theory*. Hicks himself would later criticise his 1937 paper on the grounds that it failed to take account of a number of factors crucial to the Keynesian story, including the role played by uncertainty. Nevertheless, IS/LM played a major part in getting Keynesianism into mainstream economics and still forms part of the staple diet fed to today's undergraduates.

Winning the hearts and minds of economists in Britain was a major part of the Keynesian success story. Just as important was the fight to get Keynes accepted in America, especially at the major universities, notably Harvard, and at the US Federal Reserve.

Keynes already had his supporters across the pond, notably Lorie Tarshis, who had attended his lectures at Cambridge and who in 1938 wrote *An Economic Program for American Democracy*. It received wide attention and established Tarshis as a devout Keynesian. Most importantly, from a policy perspective, it also had some influence on the US government's 1938 budget.

However, it was Alvin Hansen who was to be the standard bearer of the Keynesian message in America. He had become a professor of economics at Harvard in 1937 and, as already noted, initially had doubts about *The General Theory*. But crucially, Hansen had 'an established reputation, and he did change his mind'.[104] Hansen was also in an excellent position to influence the thinking of both current and future policy-makers, for not only would officials from Washington regularly attend his seminar at Harvard which began in September 1937 but Hansen produced a crop of students who would later take up prominent official positions. Hansen himself spent time at the Federal Reserve where he was highly effective in influencing its chairman, Marriner Eccles. Hansen's *A Guide to Keynes*, published in 1953, fully embraced the IS/LM schema.

This is not to say that Keynesian-type policies hadn't been used before the appearance of *The General Theory*. In March 1933, with the Great Depression in full swing and unemployment rising, President Roosevelt secured $3.3 billion from Congress to be spent on public works as part of his 'New Deal' programme, this despite a promise he made previously to reduce the size of the federal government (known as the 'Pittsburgh Pledge'). In line with the position espoused in *Can Lloyd George Can Do It?*, Keynes came out in support of Roosevelt's extra spending. The initiative worked, with US unemployment declining in 1934 and 1935. Further proof of the Keynesian pudding came in 1937 and 1938 when unemployment again increased, this after Roosevelt cut spending in an effort to recapture the spirit of Pittsburgh. Not long after, the economic necessities of war took over and unemployment was no longer the problem it had been.

After he had delivered his last speech at the National Mutual in February, the rest of 1938 was relatively quiet for Keynes. Much of his time was spent at Tilton, relaxing and reading some of the many books he had collected over the years. In fact, his activities as a book collector led to a minor rewriting of the history of Western philosophy. As far back as 1933, Keynes's brother Geoffrey had brought to his attention a copy of an *Abstract* of David Hume's classic *A Treatise on Human Nature*, widely believed to have been authored by a young Adam Smith and published in 1740. A textual analysis raised doubts in Keynes's mind that Smith was the author, his opinion being supported after consultations with fellow book-collector Piero Sraffa. Further investigations proved beyond doubt that the author was actually David Hume himself who, it seems, had written the *Abstract* in an attempt to publicise his *Treatise*. In March 1938, Cambridge University Press republished the pamphlet with an introduction by Keynes and Sraffa explaining their discovery.

Later in the year, Keynes again returned to his philosophical roots. In September, Tilton was the venue for a meeting of the Memoir Club, a group within Bloomsbury that had been founded in 1920. At the meeting, Keynes read out his essay 'My Early Beliefs', a reassessment of Moore's *Principia Ethica*, the book which he and his fellow Cambridge Apostles had *grown up under*. A lot had changed since then. The world had been through the shock of a world war, a conflict which the Apostles had not thought possible but one which had severely undermined the certainties of their youth. The Apostles themselves had grown up, the arrogance of their undergraduate years a distant memory. Keynes acknowledged this haughtiness in his Memoir Club paper: ... *it was exciting, exhilarating, the beginning of a renaissance, the opening of a new heaven on a new earth, we were the forerunners of a new dispensation, we were not afraid of anything*[105] and *We repudiated entirely customary morals, conventions and traditional wisdom. We were, that is to say, in the strict sense of the term, immoralists.*[106] Three decades on, Keynes still clung to Moore's 'Ideal', the notion that love, beauty and truth should come before all else. But the earlier commitment to a repudiation of anything that hinted at custom and convention had to be modified, in Keynes's opinion, as it was founded on too utopian a view of human nature and conduct. In Keynes's words, Moore and his followers did not realise that *civilization was a thin and precarious crust erected by the personality and the will of a very few.*[107] Civilisation was not the only thing that was precarious. After reading his paper, Keynes had to go and lie down, his health still a source of much trouble and concern.

The Christmas of 1938 came and went, but Keynes was still not back to his old self. Hope presented itself in March 1939 in the form of Dr Janos Plesch. Plesch was a Hungarian Jew who had escaped Germany after the Nazi takeover in 1933. Before his arrival in England, he had already treated a number of important people, including Pope Pius X and Albert Einstein who regarded Plesch as a 'swine', but also thought of him as a friend. Plesch decided to set up a surgery just off the prestigious Park Lane in London, perhaps concerned that a man of his unorthodox methods would find it hard to become established in the reputed medical district centred on Harley Street. Keynes certainly saw Plesch as out of the ordinary, describing him as *something between a quack and a genius*; Plesch's methods went some way to confirming his eccentricities. When it came to Keynes's heart problems, Plesch thought that, rather than a course of rest and relaxation, Keynes should be more active, Plesch combining this with his own unique approach, including jumping on Keynes whilst he lay in bed! For all his idiosyncrasies, the *Ogre*, as Keynes called him, seemed to have a positive impact, Keynes claiming that Plesch had brought him back to life.

His health improving, Keynes's attention began to turn to other issues. The dark clouds of war were gathering. Whilst he had been a conscientious objector during the First World War and was by nature a pacifist, he was also a realist. In August 1939 he expressed some hope that war could be averted, although it was hard to interpret Germany's massive military build up as anything but a prelude to armed aggression. Despite the fact that he had resigned from the British delegation at Versailles in 1919 and had never quite recaptured the influence within government circles he so desired, Keynes sensed that another opportunity may soon present itself.

With this in mind, he began to rebuild his spheres of influence, starting with regular attendance at his old London haunts. But simply reacquainting himself with old friends was not going to be enough. He also had to demonstrate that his views on policy were still worth listening to. *The General Theory* provided a perfect platform from which to do this. When Keynes was writing *The General Theory*, the backdrop was one of deflation and an associated lack of demand; the conditions presented by the world war were just the opposite. The combatants would have to draw on all the resources they could in order to finance military operations while at the same time trying to keep their economies on a relatively even keel. Keynes quickly realised this and set about applying the techniques contained in *The General Theory* to an economy at full employment facing the problem of excess demand. The initial result was a brace of articles published in *The Times* on 14 and 15 November 1939, where Keynes argued that if producers were unable to increase supply in conditions of full employment they would resort to increasing their prices, thereby giving rise to an 'inflationary gap'. As a solution, Keynes advocated a scheme of rationing and compulsory savings whereby people would be issued with bonds which they could redeem after the war. The spending of this money would help to counteract the slump in economic activity that was expected to follow once peace had been re-established. Keynes's ideas again attracted a considerable amount of attention and he published a refinement of his views in *How to Pay for the War*. The Treasury had also picked up on what Keynes was saying. His rehabilitation had started.

Creating a New World Order 1939–46

Although he had been out of the Treasury for many years, Keynes still had a high public profile. His views on war finance brought comments from several quarters and his ideas received further attention after a radio address on 11 March 1940. He could not be ignored, least of all by government which needed as much brain power as it could lay its hands on as it became increasingly clear that the war was not going be a short one.

Keynes's opinion of the Nazis was forthright from the beginning. He resented their utter disdain for the principles of liberal democracy and their authoritarian management of the German economy. But what could he do about it? The beginnings of an answer came towards the end of June 1940. Sir Kingsley Wood had just been appointed Chancellor of the Exchequer by Churchill. Wood, who had been trained as a solicitor and had little experience of economic matters, decided to set up a Consultative Council to advise him on war finance. Keynes was invited to join the Council, an invitation which he jumped at. He was given a room at the Treasury, from where he could observe and influence the broad sweep of economic policy.

Both Keynes and the Council had arrived too late to have any influence on the April 1940 budget presented by Wood's pro-appeasement predecessor, Sir John Simon. However, with the German invasion of the Low Countries and France in May 1940, the so-called 'Phoney War' was well and truly over and Britain's economic arrangements had to be revised accordingly. Wood presented a supplementary budget to the House of Commons on 23 July, although again it was too early for Keynes to have a major impact.

Notwithstanding Keynes's presence at the Treasury – Hubert Henderson and Dennis Robertson were there with him as was the future Governor of the Bank of England, Lord Catto – the role of economists in government, at least during the early days of the war, was somewhat limited. Although it is commonly reported that Churchill had little time for the intricacies of economic policy, he had been Chancellor for over four years in the 1920s and realised that a well-run domestic economy would play a crucial part in bolstering Britain's war effort. He suggested the expansion of the Central Economic Information Service (CEIS), which at the time reported to the Offices of the War Cabinet, and in December 1940 it was decided that the CEIS should be separated into two parts, to be known as the Central Statistical Office and the Economic Section (ES).

Recruits to the ES were usually young and thus had been heavily influenced by *The General Theory*. One of these was James Meade, who had been part of the Cambridge Circus. Meade had returned from a posting at the League of Nations in Geneva to take a job in the ES. One of his first tasks was to draw up a set of national income and expenditure accounts for use in the 1941 budget. Despite the ongoing expansion of economist numbers, the following description of the circumstances Meade found himself in at the ES shows that conditions were still far from easy: 'He [Meade] drew up a complicated and comprehensive system of balancing tables; a young Cambridge graduate in the Ministry of Economic Warfare, Richard Stone, was sent over to help him with the statistics ... Stone joined Meade in his tiny room with its single desk, established himself on a corner of the desk with a quill pen and a hand calculator, and gradually moved from the corner of the desk to the centre, while Meade turned the handle of the calculator.'[108] Ironically, Keynes believed that, in order to fulfil its remit, the Treasury would never need more than two economists.

Keynes kept a close eye on Meade and Stone's work. He had something of a vested interest as he foresaw that their calculations would play an important part in shaping budgetary policy in the years ahead but also that their work was founded on the analytical framework that he had tried to lay down in *The General Theory*. Although he was not a supporter of the use of complicated mathematical models in economics, Keynes realised that well-defined economic statistics and variables (notably private consumption and investment) were important in understanding economic processes. In *The General Theory*, he had made use of some of the earliest attempts at national income accounting, the result being the first ever estimate of the marginal propensity to consume. Whilst Meade and Stone toiled away in glorious isolation, Keynes was making his own further inroads into officialdom. After bombarding his Treasury colleagues and various members of the government with suggestions on how to run the budget, he was admitted into the Chancellor's inner circle of advisers in October 1940.

Sir Richard Stone (1913–91) attended Westminster School and Cambridge University. His work with James Meade during the Second World War laid the foundations for national income accounting as it is known today, an achievement recognised by a Nobel Prize in 1984. After the war, he served as the director of the Department of Applied Economics at Cambridge and became a Professor of Accounting and Finance.

Just a few weeks before, during the Blitz on London, Keynes, not for the first time, had a lucky escape when a bomb landed at the other end of Gordon Square. At the time, he was dining with his niece Polly and his secretary Mrs Stephens. They were

Keynes in his study in Gordon Square in 1940

unhurt, but the windows of the house were blown out and they were forced to sleep in the passage for a night. The discovery of an unexploded bomb the next morning meant that Keynes had to decamp to Tilton for a few weeks. His days were long, leaving the tranquillity of the Sussex countryside before 8am, putting in a long day's work at the Treasury, before arriving back at Tilton at around 8.30pm. Despite this, he seemed to be thriving, writing to Plesch that he got *reasonably tired, but {with} no distressing symptoms.*[109]

Back at the ES, the first results from Meade and Stone had become available in December 1940. Shortly after, Keynes circulated a copy of 'National Income, Saving and Consumption' to Treasury officials, following this up in March 1941 with the publication of an article by Meade and Stone in the *Economic Journal* summarising their findings. The most important aspect of their work was that it included, for the first time, a system of double-entry accounts for a whole country. In subsequent years, this method would for have a strong influence on the construction of national accounts throughout the world.

With the accounting framework in place, all that remained was to convince the powers that be to adopt it as part of the construction and presentation of the annual budget. This task was made easier by the fact that the level of training and knowledge of economic issues within government was relatively poor, even at the Treasury. Granted, there were some outstanding economists in the civil service, including Ralph Hawtrey, who had regularly corresponded with Keynes during the writing of *The General Theory*. But Hawtrey was an exception. Most of the mandarins could not even get close to the level of technical knowledge that the likes of Keynes and Hawtrey possessed. A good example was Wilfred Eady. He had secured a First Class degree in Classics from Cambridge and in 1942 became Second Secretary to the Treasury, this without any background in economic matters. His adviser was none other than James Meade. Eady felt at a 'disadvantage in discussions with the young professional adviser'[110] while Meade was astonished that such a situation could prevail: 'When one looks at it objectively, what a state of affairs it is when the man chiefly responsible for internal and external financial policy has had no technical training. I am sure that in our grandchildren's days this will be considered very odd.'[111]

The 1941 budget was by now rapidly approaching. Although the Meade/Stone framework was far from being the finished article, Keynes had convinced the Chancellor that it provided government and policy-makers with a more coherent framework through which to draw up and adjust fiscal policy. Wood was happy to be the messenger for this revolution in national accounting, delivering the budget on 23 July. On the policy side, Wood had also been heavily influenced by Keynes. He even went so far as to impose a level of taxation that was over and above that recommended by Keynes as being necessary to prevent the emergence of excessive levels of inflation. The gamble worked. Inflation, which had been as high as 17.2 per cent in 1940, fell significantly to 7.5 per cent in 1942. By 1943, it stood at a far more manageable 3.7 per cent, all the while against a background of steeply declining unemployment. The success that Keynes and his acolytes enjoyed in shaping official policy was remarkably rapid by the standards of the economics profession. In the space of just five years, *The General Theory* had succeeded in overhauling the way policy-makers thought of the budget.

As time went by, Keynes's contributions to budgetary policy ebbed, partly because of the success of the 1941 innovations but also because Keynes himself had moved on to other matters, in particular Britain's financial relationship with the US. In January 1941, the US Congress had approved Lend-Lease legislation. The basis of Lend-Lease was that the Americans would supply large amounts of war matériel to the Allies to assist in the war effort in exchange for US use of British overseas bases. Before its abrupt abandonment in September 1945, Lend-Lease was responsible for the distribution of over $50 billion in aid (approximately $700 billion in today's prices), the majority of which went to Britain. Other recipients included the Soviet Union, France and China.

Over the course of 1941, Keynes became more and more involved in the conduct and management of Britain's external economic policy. The first of his wartime visits to America took place in May 1941. *En route* he and Lydia dropped in on talks taking place between the British and Portuguese governments in Estoril, before boarding a plane to New York on 8 May. Two days later, Keynes was in Washington, only returning to British shores in July. This was the first of what would prove to be six trips across the Atlantic between 1941 and 1946, journeys which would severely test Keynes's mental and physical capacities.

As always with Keynes, there were many other distractions during this period, mostly at home. In the latter part of 1941, the Bank of England appointed him as one of its directors, replacing Lord Stamp who had been killed in an air raid a few months before. Keynes also continued to pursue his cultural interests, becoming a Trustee of the National Gallery in October 1941 and from February 1942, Chairman of the Council for the Encouragement of Music and the Arts (CEMA), the forerunner of today's Arts Council. In May 1942 Keynes was elevated to the peerage, becoming Lord Keynes of Tilton.

Although Keynes was absorbed with government work, the revolution he had started with *The General Theory* continued to gather pace. Cambridge was beginning to show a greater appreciation and acknowledgment of what he had achieved. In 1942 he learnt through Joan Robinson that the University was considering offering him the Professorship of Political Economy; Pigou was retiring and Keynes was the obvious replacement. Keynes doubted that he would be able to devote all his energies to the post given his precarious health and his numerous other commitments, and made it clear that he did not want to be considered, the University eventually appointing Dennis Robertson instead.

Keynes's decision was also driven by his belief that *The General Theory* had achieved its task of converting Cambridge students to a new way of thinking about economics. Pigou for one was aware of alleged 'brainwashing', especially of undergraduates.

Describing the answers to that year's Economics Tripos questions, Pigou wrote to Keynes in June 1940 that, 'The chief bad thing ... we ... found was that a very large number of people had been stuffed like sausages with bits of your stuff in such a way that (1) they were quite incapable of applying their own intelligence to it, and (2) they perpetually dragged it in regardless of its relevance to the question ... My own guess ... is that the parrot-like treatment of your stuff is due to the lectures and supervision of the beautiful Mrs Robinson – a magpie breeding innumerable parrots.'[112]

Within Whitehall, there was further confirmation at the end of 1942 of the deep impact made by the 'Keynesian Revolution' with the publication of an investigation into Britain's social security arrangements entitled *Social Insurance and Allied Services*, otherwise known as the Beveridge Report, after its author William Beveridge. The report implicitly assumed that government would be able to manipulate demand along Keynesian lines in the post-war period, thereby maintaining full employment, defined by Beveridge as being less than 3 per cent unemployment. This, in turn, would help to finance an expansion of welfare provision for those who, for whatever reason, were unable to work. The newly-elected Labour government of 1945 embraced Beveridge's recommendations and announced the creation of a National Health Service (although it would take until 1948 to get the new system up and running) and a deepening of benefit provision which would protect individuals from the 'cradle to the grave'. The emphasis on full employment continued in Beveridge's *Full Employment in a Free Society* and the British government's White Paper on Employment Policy, both of which were published in 1944.

Keynes could look on these developments with some satisfaction. In the space of a few years, he had succeeded in influencing official and popular opinion to an extent which most economists could only dream about. But Keynes was never one to dwell on such matters. His country now needed him to make the necessary arrangements which would enable it to get through what was turning out to be an increasingly costly war. Part of the problem lay in the fact that Britain's trade balance with the rest of the world was suffering due to a marked weakening of exports on the one hand and the need to keep importing large amounts of goods that could not be produced at home on the other. Overseas assets even had to be sold to maintain solvency.

For his part, Keynes believed that Britain should be compensated for the leading role it had assumed in the war before the entry of the Americans. But Washington had its own agenda. Before 1939, the existence of the British Empire meant that a large portion of the world economy was controlled from London, often to the exclusion of other countries. In other words, a 'Sterling Area' emerged, whereby the pound sterling could not be converted into other currencies but rather could only be spent in another country that had either adopted the pound or pegged its currency to the pound. The Americans saw this as grossly unfair and detrimental to the efficient functioning of the world economy. With its own economic power rapidly strengthening, Washington took the opportunity presented by the war to press the British to open up its Empire markets.

At a broader level, the international monetary system needed some serious repair. In 1941 Keynes had already foreseen that change would be needed in the post-war period and, to this end, he drew up the first of many drafts of a proposal he initially called an 'International Currency Union', subsequently renamed an 'International Clearing Union' and colloquially known as the 'Keynes Plan'. Keynes advocated the introduction of a new reserve currency, which he named 'bancor'. He proposed that each country would be issued with bancor accounts which would be administered by an international central bank. The value of these accounts would be related to the value of a country's own currency. The overriding objective was for each country to run a zero or near-zero balance on its bancor account. By doing so, the problems associated with significant bilateral trade imbalances could be avoided. Whenever a country built up a trade surplus or deficit, it would be required to adjust its exchange rate accordingly to remove the imbalance. By early 1942, the Keynes Plan had already gone through four drafts and was receiving an increasing level of support in Whitehall.[113]

Meanwhile, financial negotiations between the British and US governments went on incessantly throughout the second half of the war, Keynes shouldering much of the strain on the British side. There was some respite from the talks. Whenever he was in Washington, Keynes liked to stay at the Mayflower Hotel where he enjoyed the tranquillity of the Coffee Shop. His nephew, Quentin, who was posted in Washington at the time, would regularly take him out for drives and long walks. Keynes would also visit the cinema, and when in New York, would go to the ballet and the Museum of Modern Art.[114] There was also time to catch up with old acquaintances, such as Albert Einstein whom Keynes had met previously in Berlin. At Princeton in June 1943, Keynes and Lydia found the great physicist 'in bed with the curly hair and the big toe out'.[115] They also socialised with Lord Halifax, who had become Britain's Ambassador to the US in 1940. Maynard and Lydia spent the presidential election night of 1944 with him at the British Embassy, all of them thoroughly entertained by the conversational brilliance of another guest, the philosopher Isaiah Berlin.[116]

Keynes's personal relations with the Americans were sometimes frosty, driven by the impatience of his mind as well as a growing physical exhaustion. The treacherous sea crossings didn't help. In spite of his physical ailments, Keynes's mental acumen was little dented and he dominated the ongoing talks. Even shortly before the landmark conference at Bretton Woods when Keynes was near the point of collapse, his magnetic personality continued to shine through. At a meeting between British and American officials at

Atlantic City in June 1944, Keynes's old sparring partner, Lionel Robbins, who was part of the British delegation and who had grown closer to Keynes since the Cambridge-LSE rivalry of the early 1930s, was spellbound: 'In the late afternoon we had a joint session with the Americans ... This went very well indeed. Keynes was in his most lucid and persuasive mood; and the effect was irresistible. At such moments, I often find myself thinking that Keynes must be one of the most remarkable men that have ever lived – the quick logic, the birdlike swoop of intuition, the vivid fancy, the wide vision, above all the incomparable sense of the fitness of words, all combine to make something several degrees beyond the limit of ordinary human achievement. Certainly, in our own age, only the Prime Minister is of comparable stature ... The Americans sat entranced as the God-like visitor sang and the golden light played around.'[117]

With such a force of personality on their side, the British could have been forgiven for thinking that the Keynes Plan would win the day. They didn't count on Harry Dexter White (1892–1948). White was a trained economist who had been appointed Special Assistant to the Secretary of the Treasury in 1942 and Assistant Secretary of the Treasury in 1945. As a result, he was in charge of America's financial negotiations with Britain. Like Keynes, White had been working on his own plan for international trade. He was of the view that any revision to monetary arrangements should be sympathetic to the economic superpower status of the US and, where possible, support it in this role. The 'White Plan' therefore proposed that the US dollar (along with gold) should be at the centre of a new monetary order, not Keynes's bancor. In parallel, White supported the creation of a so-called 'International Stabilisation Fund of United and Associated Nations' which would help to promote trade by holding quotas of gold and other currencies in reserve for each of its members. But it would stop short of becoming the 'world bank' envisaged by Keynes. All of this

Harry Dexter White (left) and Keynes at the Bretton Woods Conference

would be underpinned by a system of 'pegged' currency regimes, whereby countries would declare a par value for their currency and could intervene to limit sizeable movements in this value.

It soon became clear that Washington's power and influence meant that the White Plan, with its heavy emphasis on price stability over economic growth, held the upper hand going into the final round of meetings held in July 1944 between the Americans, the British and the other Allied nations at the Mount Washington Hotel at Bretton Woods in New Hampshire. For a gruelling three weeks, the British, led by Keynes, and the Americans, headed by White, dominated the conference's proceedings, discussing and arguing over the minutiae of how the post-war world economy should be run. There were real fears that Keynes's health might not stand up to the pressure of the very long hours, fears which were partly confirmed when he suffered a minor heart attack on 19 July after running up some stairs too quickly in an effort to get to a committee meeting on time. Luckily, the conference was nearly at an end.

As expected, the final agreement adopted by the delegates was heavily influenced by White. A system of pegged currencies was approved and the International Monetary Fund (IMF) was established to help foster international trade. It would assign quotas to each of its members based on the size of a country's economy relative to the world economy. In turn, the quota would determine how much financial assistance a member country could expect to receive from the IMF if it got into balance of payments difficulties. Bretton Woods also created the World Bank and the General Agreement on Tariffs and Trade (GATT), the forerunner of today's World Trade Organisation (WTO). Although the Americans had got their way at Bretton Woods, the delegates still looked on Keynes as something of a hero. Just after he had delivered his farewell address and was about to leave the room, they rose out of their seats and burst into a chorus of 'For He's a Jolly Good Fellow'.[118]

Keynes's work in America was still not done. Britain still needed American financial assistance to avoid a balance of payments crisis and a wider economic meltdown after the war. As noted, Keynes thought that Britain should be given a substantial amount of money by the US in order to see it through the early years of peace. Keynes had originally asked Washington for $6 billion. After indications emerged that this was unrealistically high, discussions centred on a revised figure of between $3–4 billion. The new President, Harry Truman, settled the debate, approving a final figure of $3.75 billion. This was to be in the form of a loan, not a gift,[119] with Canada stumping up a further $1.25 billion. In return, Washington demanded that the Sterling Area be opened up to third-country trade, a demand that Britain had no choice but to agree to. Keynes also secured a further loan of $586 million from the Americans to be used to pay for any equipment which was left over in Britain or which was in transit after the abrupt termination of Lend-Lease in early September 1945. The terms of these two loans were extraordinarily generous, no doubt reflecting Washington's satisfaction at breaking open the Sterling Area: the US would charge a fixed interest rate of just 2 per cent and the repayment period was set at 50 annual instalments starting in 1950. After missing six payments because of various financial difficulties, the British government finally paid off this debt in December 2006.

Keynes's war work was at last done. All that remained was to pay a courtesy call on President Truman in Washington on 7 May before leaving New York on the *Queen Elizabeth* bound for home a few days later. He arrived back in Britain on 17 December, just in time to take part in a debate in the House of Lords on Bretton Woods and the loan negotiations.[120] Keynes's timing was perfect: although there had been domestic concerns over the loan agreements in particular, a brilliant speech by Keynes convinced their Lordships that what had been decided upon in America was in Britain's best economic interests, at least over the short term.

And what became of Harry Dexter White? In 1946 he was made an Executive Director of the IMF, also serving as Acting Managing Director for a while. Suffering from ill health, he resigned from the Fund in June 1947. Shortly after, he was accused of being a Soviet spy, although he denied all such claims; the balance of evidence appears to suggest that White was not, in fact, working for the Soviets. With his health in serious decline, White died of a heart attack in August 1948.

'He Died for his Country' 1946

Back in Britain for the Christmas of 1945, Keynes had a lot of catching-up to do, not only with his friends but also his health, which had taken a battering in America. Much of the festive period was spent at Tilton where Keynes re-established contact with Charleston and Leonard Woolf, still terribly lonely after the death of Virginia in 1941. It was much like old times, with the former Bloomsberries once again enjoying each other's company and gossip.

Keynes also still had ties with Cambridge. The war had disrupted his attendance at the Political Economy Club, but he was still its star attraction when he read out a paper on the US dollar in early February 1946. Dennis Robertson was now in the chair, although he was of course outshone by Keynes, who despite his frailty gave a sparkling performance. It would be his last visit to his beloved Cambridge.

Much of the rest of early 1946 was taken up by preparations for the re-opening of the Royal Opera House in Covent Garden. Keynes had been appointed Chairman of the Board of Trustees and so was intimately involved in the process of converting the building which had been used as a dance hall during the war into something that would again be suitable for opera and ballet. The opening night was set for 20 February, with an extravagant performance of *The Sleeping Beauty*. Margot Fonteyn would perform the part of the Princess and Robert Helpmann would be the Prince.

The stage designs were by Oliver Messel and Karl Rankl was the music director. The guest list was just as impressive, headed as it was by King George VI and Queen Elizabeth and their two daughters, Princesses Elizabeth (the present Queen) and Margaret. Everything was set for a grand occasion and Keynes must have been happy that the pressures of war were over both for him and for Britain. But all was not well with his health. He had been due to take part in the greeting party that would welcome the royals but fell ill at the last moment. He had to retire to his box, leaving Lydia to fill in. Although he recovered enough to enjoy the evening's performance, it was another stark reminder of his physical weakness.[121]

There was also to be one last crossing of the Atlantic. The day before the Royal Opera House opened its doors, Keynes had been appointed Britain's Governor of both the IMF and the World Bank. He was thus obliged to attend the inaugural meetings of the two institutions which were due to take place in the middle of March at Savannah, Georgia. The journey was a long one. Maynard and Lydia set out on the *Queen Mary* bound for New York on 24 February, not arriving at their destination until 1 March. Surprisingly, Keynes's health held up reasonably well. After frantic socialising in New York, the couple decided to spend a few days in Washington. Whilst there, Keynes met the new Secretary of the Treasury, Fred Vinson. Vinson made it clear to Keynes that both the IMF and the World Bank would be located in Washington, not New York as Keynes had advocated. The US government wanted to keep a close political eye on the two institutions, regarding any economic synergies that the Fund and the Bank would have benefited from by being in America's financial capital as being of only secondary importance. Vinson was also in favour of the IMF having full-time, highly paid directors, contrary to a British wish for directors to be part-time with a lower salary.

Keynes felt frustrated. The Americans had already played the dominant role at Bretton Woods and had secured greater access to the Sterling Area. Agreeing to British proposals over the location of the IMF and the World Bank and the make up the IMF's senior staff did not seem like too much to ask and would, if agreed to, signal Washington's flexibility when it came to the administration of the new institutions. However, there was to be no movement when the parties reached Savannah. The American proposals were adopted, leaving Keynes upset and depressed. On the night train back to Washington, he was again struck down with chest pains, his life hanging in the balance for two hours. Although he eventually recovered and was able to make the long trip home, he was now living on borrowed time.

On his return to Britain, an extended period of rest and relaxation would surely have done him some good. But he continued to plough on, and by early April his appointments diary was again full. He still had commitments at the Treasury and the Bank of England, dinner dates here and there, and extensive involvement in various arts projects. Any rest that was to be had was at Tilton, where he would indulge his passion for reading some of the many books he had collected over the years, especially those from the Elizabethan period, which he had a particular liking for. Another of his pastimes was to go for long walks across the Sussex Downs, his favourite spot being the top of Firle Beacon, just above Tilton. In years gone by, he could climb it without assistance. Now he had to use a car.

As Easter 1946 approached, Keynes's health enjoyed something of an improvement. On Saturday 20 April he drove to the top of Firle Beacon, accompanied by Lydia and his mother Florence. The weather was magnificent; the view must have been beautiful. Keynes was in a buoyant mood. For the first time in years, he decided to walk down the path that led to his home. He and Lydia disappeared down the hill, watched by his mother, who had opted to descend by car. But the strain proved too much. The next morning, Easter Sunday, he suffered a massive heart attack whilst lying in bed. Maynard Keynes was dead, aged just 62.

In the days and weeks that followed, Lydia was inundated with messages of condolence from far and wide. Robbins remarked how Keynes had 'given his life for his country, as surely as if he had fallen on the field of battle',[122] whilst Hayek claimed that Keynes was 'the only great man I ever knew, and for whom I had unbounded admiration'.[123] As a mark of the high esteem in which his country held him, a memorial service was held at Westminster Abbey. Both of his parents were there; Churchill would have been had he not been unavoidably called away on foreign business. Keynes's body was cremated. He had wanted his ashes to be placed in the vault at King's College, but his brother Geoffrey, either forgetting this last wish or ignoring it, scattered them on the hills above Tilton.

Keynes's material legacy was substantial. His various investment activities meant that his estate was valued at just under £480,000 at the time of his death, the equivalent of around £13 million in today's money. His library was also impressive, containing about 4,000 volumes, numerous books on economics and around 300 manuscripts. He had a particular liking for Sir Isaac Newton and possessed what was probably the largest private collection of Newton's work anywhere in the world.[124] Keynes's library was split between King's College and the Marshall

Sir Isaac Newton (1642–1727), was one of the greatest scientists of his or any other time, making fundamental contributions to both physics and mathematics. Keynes described Newton as Cambridge's *greatest son*. However, he disagreed with the traditional view that Newton was the first great scientist of the age of reason. Rather, Keynes saw Newton as *the last of the magicians, the last of the Babylonians and Sumerians, the last great mind which looked out on the visible and intellectual world with the same eyes as those who began to build our intellectual inheritance rather less than 10,000 years ago.*

Keynes's London house, 46 Gordon Square, as it is today. Note the blue plaque

Library of Economics at Cambridge. For her part, Lydia carried on living at Tilton, becoming increasingly reclusive. She outlived her eminent husband by 35 years, dying in 1981. Her ashes were scattered on the same spot as Maynard's, all those years ago.

What happened to the Keynesian Revolution? One of the driving forces behind the success of *The General Theory* was the sheer power of Keynes's personality and his infectious optimism. Although not aggressive, he also had an oral and written mastery of the English language that was almost unrivalled. This, combined with the musicality of his voice, made his ideas all the more believable. With Keynes gone, some of the vitality behind the revolution that he had started inevitably disappeared. Nevertheless, the power and originality of *The General Theory* meant that Keynes's ideas still had some way to run.

The new macroeconomics received some of its greatest support from the writers of economics textbooks. The most important breakthrough took place in 1948 with the appearance of Paul Samuelson's *Economics: An Introductory Analysis*. Samuelson based the book on his invention of the so-called 'Keynesian cross diagram', a simple representation of the relationship between saving, investment and national income. As a testament to the longevity of Samuelson's analysis, *Economics* remains in print today and has gone through 18 editions. With over four million copies sold, it is by far and away the most successful economics textbook ever written.

Much of the post-war prosperity enjoyed by the industrialised nations up until the 1973 oil crisis was credited to the adoption of Keynesian ideas, although this continues to be hotly debated. It is certainly true that *The General Theory* had made such an impact upon publication that post-war economists, many of whom had been students in the mid-1930s and were thus swept up in the Keynesian avalanche, could hardly escape its influence. The revolution in national accounting that Keynes had helped to oversee, at least in Britain, also played a role in underpinning the case for 'Keynesianism' in the post-war era.

However, matters started to unravel in the early 1970s. In August 1971, the Bretton Woods system of pegged exchange rates was abandoned as a result of President Nixon's decision to allow the US dollar to float on the back of concerns that America's trade performance was beginning to deteriorate. But the real crunch came in 1973 when the OPEC countries hiked oil prices. What emerged was a simultaneous increase in unemployment and inflation. Keynesianism could cope with one or the other, but not both; 'The Age of Keynes' was over.

Paul Samuelson (b. 1915) has made important contributions across a variety of subject areas within economics, including mathematical economics, international trade theory and consumer theory. He has been based at the Massachusetts Institute of Technology (MIT) since 1940 and was an adviser to Presidents Kennedy and Johnson. In 1970, Samuelson became the first American to receive the Nobel Prize in Economics.

Economists quickly began to look around for other explanations of the business cycle. The most successful of these was the monetarist theories associated with the US economist Milton Friedman. Friedman saw inflation as the main problem facing modern economies, arguing, in line with the quantity theory, that it could be tamed if the monetary authorities kept a tight rein on the money supply. Although he did not give it primacy, Keynes himself was certainly aware of the fact that price stability should be an important objective for policy-makers and that this could be achieved through money supply controls. Meanwhile, the rise of Friedman and the monetarists had received official sanction due to the adoption of their ideas by the Thatcher and Reagan governments. Friedman was also a supporter of a reduction in the size of government, a position pounced on by the Conservatives in Britain who used it as the justification for a vast programme of privatisation. Despite all this, Keynesianism continued to do the rounds, the Thatcher government often running budget deficits.

A whole host of other business cycle theories have sprung up subsequently, going by a variety of names including the influential New Classical Macroeconomics, based on the idea that individuals possess 'rational expectations' about how the economy works and stressing the importance of modelling the process by which economic agents forecast future events; real business cycle theory; New Keynesianism; and Post-Keynesianism to mention a few. One can only wonder how policy-makers are expected to distil the best aspects of each theory in order to produce optimal policy decisions. Indeed, it could be argued that economists have been led astray by this preponderance of competing theories, at the same time becoming obsessed by mathematical sophistication at the expense of policy relevance. Keynes would have winced. However, it will take another Keynes to bring it all together.

Notes

1. Roy F Harrod, *The Life of John Maynard Keynes* (Macmillan, London: 1951) p 10, hereafter Harrod, *Keynes*.

2. Robert Skidelsky, *John Maynard Keynes. Volume 1: Hopes Betrayed 1883-1920* (Macmillan, London: 1983), p 13, hereafter Skidelsky, *Hopes Betrayed*.

3. Diaries of John Neville Keynes, held at Cambridge University Library: 24 October 1894 (library reference MS Add 7844), 2 November 1894 (MS Add 7844) and 11 December 1899 (MS Add 7849). Reproduced here by permission of the Syndics of Cambridge University Library.

4. Goodchild quoted in Harrod, *Keynes*, p 13.

5. John Maynard Keynes to John Neville Keynes, 30 April 1899, in Harrod, *Keynes*, p 19.

6. Harrod, *Keynes*, p 36.

7. Keynes to Keynes, late (26 or 27) July 1902, in the Keynes Papers held at King's College, Cambridge. Hereafter referred to as KP followed by the folder reference: KP/PP/45/168/6/277-278.

8. Skidelsky, *Hopes Betrayed*, p 106.

9. Bertrand Russell, *The Autobiography of Bertrand Russell* (George Allen & Unwin Ltd., London: 1967) p 72.

10. Alfred Marshall to John Neville Keynes, 3 December 1905, in Harrod, *Keynes*, p 107.

11. John Maynard Keynes to Lytton Strachey, 15 November 1905, in Skidelsky, *Hopes Betrayed*, p 165.

12. Keynes to Strachey, 4 October 1906, in *The Collected Writings of John Maynard Keynes, Volume XV: Activities 1906-14: India and Cambridge*, ed. Elizabeth Johnson (Macmillan St Martin's Press for the Royal Economic Society: 1971) pp 2–3.

13. Keynes to Strachey, 13 September 1907, in Harrod, *Keynes*, p 123.

14. Alfred North Whitehead, 1909, in KP/TP/4/8.

15. Skidelsky, *Hopes Betrayed*, p 184.

16. John Neville Keynes quoted in John Maloney, *Marshall, Orthodoxy and the Professionalisation of Economics* (Cambridge University Press: 1985) p 64.

17. Keynes to Duncan Grant, 19 January 1909, in Harrod, *Keynes*, p 147.

18. Austin Robinson, 'John Maynard Keynes 1883-1946', *Economic Journal*, 57 (1947) p 27.

19. Keynes to Keynes, October 1911(?), in Skidelsky, *Hopes Betrayed*, p 207.

20. *The Spectator* (supplement), 1 November 1913, in KP/IC/9/2-3.

21. Keynes to Strachey, 27 November 1914, in Harrod, *Keynes*, p 200.

22. *The Collected Writings of John Maynard Keynes, Volume XVI: Activities 1914-19: The Treasury and Versailles*, ed. Elizabeth Johnson (Macmillan St Martin's Press for the Royal Economic Society: 1971) p 178.

23. *The Collected Writings of John Maynard Keynes, Volume XVI: Activities 1914-19: The Treasury and Versailles*, p 3.

24. See Kathleen Burk, 'The Diplomacy of Finance: British Financial Missions to the United States 1914-1918', *Historical Journal*, 22 (1979) p 358.

25. Harry G Johnson, 'The Early Economics of Keynes', *American Economic Review*, 62 (1972) (Papers and Proceedings) p 419.

26. See David Scrase and Peter Croft, *Maynard Keynes: Collector of pictures, books and manuscripts* (Provost and Scholars of King's College, Cambridge: 1983) p 19.

27. *The Collected Writings of John Maynard Keynes, Volume II: The Economic Consequences of the Peace* (Macmillan St Martin's Press for the Royal Economic Society: 1971) p 174.

28. *The Collected Writings of John Maynard Keynes, Volume II: The Economic Consequences of the Peace*, p 90.

29. *The Collected Writings of John Maynard Keynes, Volume II: The Economic Consequences of the Peace*, p 89.

30. Keynes to David Lloyd George, 5 June 1919, in Harrod, *Keynes*, p 253.

31. Don Patinkin, *Anticipations of the General Theory? And Other Essays on Keynes* (Basil Blackwell, Oxford: 1982) p 33.

32. *The Collected Writings of John Maynard Keynes, Volume II: The Economic Consequences of the Peace*, p 1.

33. *The Collected Writings of John Maynard Keynes, Volume II: The Economic Consequences of the Peace*, p 18.

34. *The Collected Writings of John Maynard Keynes, Volume II: The Economic Consequences of the Peace*, p 19.

35. *The Collected Writings of John Maynard Keynes, Volume II: The Economic Consequences of the Peace*, p 20.

36. *The Collected Writings of John Maynard Keynes, Volume X: Essays in Biography* (Macmillan St Martin's Press for the Royal Economic Society: 1972) p 23.

37. *The Collected Writings of John Maynard Keynes, Volume II: The Economic Consequences of the Peace*, p 26.

38. *The Collected Writings of John Maynard Keynes, Volume II: The Economic Consequences of the Peace*, p 25.

39. *The Collected Writings of John Maynard Keynes, Volume II: The Economic Consequences of the Peace*, pp 25–7.

40. See review of Étienne Mantoux's *The Carthaginian Peace, or the Economic Consequences of Mr. Keynes*, by Michael A Heilperin in *American Economic Review*, 36 (1946) p 933.

41. Harrod, *Keynes*, p 283.

42. Robert Skidelsky, *John Maynard Keynes. Volume 2: The Economist as Saviour, 1920-1937* (Macmillan, London: 1992) p 19, hereafter Skidelsky, *The Economist as Saviour*.

43. Austin Robinson, 'John Maynard Keynes 1883-1946', *Economic Journal*, 57 (1947) p 26.

44. See *The Collected Writings of John Maynard Keynes, Volume XII: Economic Articles and Correspondence: Investment and Editorial*, ed. Donald Moggridge (Macmillan Cambridge University Press for the Royal Economic Society: 1983) p 11.

45. See *The Collected Writings of John Maynard Keynes, Volume XII: Economic Articles and Correspondence: Investment and Editorial*, pp 89–90.

46. See *The Collected Writings of John Maynard Keynes, Volume XII: Economic Articles and Correspondence: Investment and Editorial*, pp 10–11.

47. *The Collected Writings of John Maynard Keynes, Volume IV: A Tract on Monetary Reform* (Macmillan St Martin's Press for the Royal Economic Society: 1971) p 65.

48. See Steven B Webb, *Hyperinflation and Stabilization in Weimar Germany* (Oxford University Press, New York: 1989) p 3.

49. Vanessa Bell to Keynes, 20 May 1922, in Victoria Glendinning, *Leonard Woolf* (Simon & Schuster: 2006) p 249.

50. Skidelsky, *The Economist as Saviour*, p 285.

51. *The Collected Writings of John Maynard Keynes, Volume V: A Treatise on Money, 1 The Pure Theory of Money* (Macmillan St Martin's Press for the Royal Economic Society: 1971) p xvii.

52. Keynes to Florence Ada Keynes, 14 September 1930, in *The Collected Writings of John Maynard Keynes, Volume V A Treatise on Money, 1 The Pure Theory of Money*, p xv.

53. *The Collected Writings of John Maynard Keynes, Volume V A Treatise on Money, 1 The Pure Theory of Money*, p xvii.

54. *The Collected Writings of John Maynard Keynes, Volume XX: Activities 1929-31: Rethinking Employment and Unemployment Policies*, ed. Donald Moggridge (Macmillan Cambridge University Press for the Royal Economic Society: 1981) p 17.

55. Keynes to Ramsay MacDonald, 10 July 1930, in *The Collected Writings of John Maynard Keynes, Volume XX: Activities 1929-31: Rethinking Employment and Unemployment Policies*, p 369.

56. *The Collected Writings of John Maynard Keynes, Volume IX: Essays in Persuasion* (Macmillan St Martin's Press for the Royal Economic Society: 1972) p xvii.

57. Lionel Robbins, *An Essay on the Nature and Significance of Economic Science*, 2nd edition, revised and extended (Macmillan, London: 1952) p 16.

58. Arakie quoted in Alan Ebenstein, *Friedrich Hayek. A Biography* (University of Chicago Press, Chicago and London: 2003) p 74.

59. Ebenstein, *Friedrich Hayek. A Biography*, p 63.

60. See Donald Markwell, *John Maynard Keynes and International Relations* (Oxford University Press: 2006) pp 9–10.

61. Friedrich August von Hayek, 'Reflections on the Pure Theory of Money of Mr. J.M. Keynes', *Economica*, 33 (1931) p 270.

62. *The Collected Writings of John Maynard Keynes, Volume XIII: The General Theory and After: Part I, Preparation*, ed. Donald Moggridge (Macmillan St Martin's Press for the Royal Economic Society: 1973) p 243.

63. John Maynard Keynes, 'The Pure Theory of Money: A Reply to Dr. Hayek' *Economica*, 34 (1931) p 387.

64. Keynes, 'The Pure Theory of Money: A Reply to Dr. Hayek', p 394.

65. Piero Sraffa, 'Dr. Hayek on Money and Capital', *Economic Journal*, 42 (1932) p 45.

66. Keynes quoted in George C Peden, 'Keynes and British economic policy', Chapter 6 in *The Cambridge Companion to Keynes*, ed. Roger E Backhouse and Bradley W Bateman (Cambridge University Press: 2006) p 106.

67. Skidelsky, *The Economist as Saviour*, p 287.

68. See Maria C Marcuzzo, 'The Collaboration between J.M Keynes and R.F. Kahn from the Treatise to the General Theory', *History of Political Economy*, 34 (2002) p 422.

69. Keynes to Richard Kahn, 24 March 1933, in *The Collected Writings of John Maynard Keynes, Volume XIII: The General Theory and After: Part I, Preparation*, p 413.

70. Keynes to Joan Robinson, 8 June 1935, in *The Collected Writings of John Maynard Keynes, Volume XIII: The General Theory and After: Part I, Preparation*, p 638.

71. Austin Robinson, 'Keynes and his Cambridge Colleagues', Chapter 3 in *Keynes, Cambridge and the General Theory*, ed. Don Patinkin and J Clark Leith (Macmillan, London: 1977) p 33.

72. Peter Clarke, *The Keynesian Revolution and its Economic Consequences. Selected Essays by Peter Clarke* (Edward Elgar: 1998) p 89.

73. Joan Robinson, 'Misunderstandings in the theory of production', *Greek Economic Review*, 1 (1979) p 1.

74. See George R Feiwel, 'Joan Robinson Inside and Outside the Stream', Chapter 1 in *Joan Robinson and Modern Economic Theory* ed. George R Feiwel (Macmillan, Basingstoke: 1989) p 39.

75. *The Collected Writings of John Maynard Keynes, Volume XIII: The General Theory and After: Part I, Preparation*, p 342.

76. See *The Collected Writings of John Maynard Keynes, Volume XIII: The General Theory and After: Part I, Preparation*, p 343.

77. Keynes to Robinson, 29 March 1934, in *The Collected Writings of John Maynard Keynes, Volume XIII: The General Theory and After: Part I, Preparation*, p 422.

78. Franklin Roosevelt to Felix Frankfurter, 11 June 1934, in Harrod, *Keynes*, p 448.

79. Keynes quoted in Harrod, *Keynes*, p 20.

80. Keynes to George Bernard Shaw, 1 January 1935, in *The Collected Writings of John Maynard Keynes, Volume XIII: The General Theory and After: Part I, Preparation*, pp 492–3.

81. See Harrod, *Keynes*, p 474.

82. Paul A Samuelson, 'Lord Keynes and the General Theory', *Econometrica*, 14 (1946) p 190.

83. *The Collected Writings of John Maynard Keynes, Volume VII: The General Theory of Employment, Interest and Money*, (Macmillan Cambridge University Press for the Royal Economic Society: 1973) p xxiii.

84. *The Collected Writings of John Maynard Keynes, Volume VII: The General Theory of Employment, Interest and Money*, p xxii.

85. *The Collected Writings of John Maynard Keynes, Volume VII: The General Theory of Employment, Interest and Money*, pp 383–4

86. See Harrod, *Keynes*, p 478.

87. Keynes to Lydia Keynes, 3 May 1936, in *The Collected Writings of John Maynard Keynes, Volume XXIX: The General*

Theory and After: A Supplement, ed. Donald Moggridge (Macmillan Cambridge University Press for the Royal Economic Society: 1979) p 218.

88. See *Contemporary Responses to the General Theory*, ed. Roger E Backhouse (St. Augustine's Press, South Bend, Indiana: 1999) p 2.

89. Arthur C Pigou, 'Mr. J.M. Keynes' General Theory of Employment, Interest and Money', *Economica*, 3 (1936) p 115.

90. Alvin H Hansen, 'Under-Employment Equilibrium', *Yale Review*, 25 (1936) p 829.

91. Alvin H Hansen, 'Mr Keynes on Underemployment Equilibrium', *Journal of Political Economy*, 44 (1936) p 686.

92. Hansen, 'Mr Keynes on Underemployment Equilibrium', p 686.

93. George L S Shackle, *The Years of High Theory* (Cambridge University Press, Cambridge: 1967) p 296.

94. See John K Galbraith, 'How Keynes came to America', Chapter 2 in *Keynesianism and the Keynesian Revolution in America*, ed. O F Hamouda and B B Price (Edward Elgar, Cheltenham: 1998) p 11.

95. Donald Winch, *Economics and Policy. A Historical Study* (Hodder and Stoughton: 1969) p 177.

96. John Maynard Keynes, 'The General Theory of Employment', *Quarterly Journal of Economics*, 51 (1937) p 213.

97. Keynes to Lydia Keynes, 24 January 1937, in Skidelsky, *The Economist as Saviour*, p 629.

98. *The Collected Writings of John Maynard Keynes, Volume XXI: Activities 1931-39: World Crises and Policies in Britain and America*, ed. Donald Moggridge (Macmillan Cambridge University Press for the Royal Economic Society: 1982) p 413.

99. Keynes to Roy Harrod, 30 August 1936, in *The Collected Writings of John Maynard Keynes, Volume XIV: The General Theory and After: Part II, Defence and Development*, ed. Donald Moggridge (Macmillan St Martin's Press for the Royal Economic Society: 1973) p 85.

100. Kahn to Harrod, 13 November 1934, in the Kahn Papers at King's College, Cambridge. Folder reference: RFK/13/57/70.

101. Keynes to Abba Lerner, 16 June 1936, in *The Collected Writings of John Maynard Keynes, Volume XXIX: The General Theory and After: A Supplement*, pp 214 and 216.

102. Lerner quoted in Harry Landreth and David C Colander, *History of Economic Thought*, 2nd edition (Houghton Mifflin Company, 1989) p 359.

103. Keynes to Harold Macmillan, 27 April 1932, in *The Collected Writings of John Maynard Keynes, Volume XII: Economic Articles and Correspondence: Investment and Editorial*, p 861.

104. Galbraith, 'How Keynes came to America', p 12.

105. *The Collected Writings of John Maynard Keynes, Volume X: Essays in Biography*, p 435.

106. *The Collected Writings of John Maynard Keynes, Volume X: Essays in Biography*, p 446.

107. *The Collected Writings of John Maynard Keynes, Volume X: Essays in Biography*, p 447.

108. 'James Meade' by Susan Howson in the *Oxford Dictionary of National Biography*, http://www.oxforddnb.com

109. Keynes to Janos Plesch, September(?) 1940, in Harrod, *Keynes*, p 501.

110. Clarke, *The Keynesian Revolution and its Economic Consequences. Selected Essays by Peter Clarke*, p 170.

111. Meade quoted in Clarke, *The Keynesian Revolution and its Economic Consequences. Selected Essays by Peter Clarke*, p 170.

112. Pigou quoted in Robert Skidelsky, *John Maynard Keynes. Volume 3: Fighting for Freedom, 1937-1946* (Macmillan, London: 2000) p 77, hereafter Skidelsky, *Fighting for Freedom*.

113. See Donald E. Moggridge, 'Keynes and his correspondence', Chapter 8 in *The Cambridge Companion to Keynes*, p 148.

114. See Harrod, *Keynes*, p 556.

115. Lydia Keynes quoted in Skidelsky, *Fighting for Freedom*, p 120.

116. See Harrod, *Keynes*, p 591.

117. *The Wartime Diaries of Lionel Robbins and James Meade, 1943-45*, ed. Susan Howson and Donald Moggridge (Macmillan, Basingstoke: 1990) pp 158–9.

118. See Harrod, *Keynes*, p 584.

119. See Harrod, *Keynes*, pp 610–11.

120. See *The Collected Writings of John Maynard Keynes, Volume XXIV: Activities 1944-46: The Transition to Peace*, ed. Donald Moggridge (Macmillan Cambridge University Press for the Royal Economic Society: 1979) p 605.

121. See Harrod, *Keynes*, pp 622–3.

122. Robbins quoted in Skidelsky, *Fighting for Freedom,* p 472.

123. Hayek quoted in Skidelsky, *Fighting for Freedom,* p 472.

124. See Harrod, *Keynes*, pp 483–4.

Year	Age	Life
1883		5 June: John Maynard Keynes born at 6 Harvey Road, Cambridge.
1889	6	Keynes attends his first school, the Perse School Kindergarten in Cambridge.
1892	9	January: Keynes starts at St Faith's Preparatory School in Cambridge.
1897	14	July: Sits the Eton College entrance examination, securing a place as 'Tenth King's Scholar'. September: begins at Eton.
1898	15	Wins ten prizes in his first year at Eton. Comes under the influence of Samuel Lubbock.
1901	18	Wins Eton's prestigious Tomline and Chamberlayne Prizes.
1902	19	Enters King's College, Cambridge, after winning a scholarship to read mathematics. Makes debut speech at the Cambridge Union.
1903	20	February: Becomes member number 243 of the Apostles. November: Defends the cause of free trade at the Cambridge Union.
1904	21	Becomes close friends with Lytton Strachey. Elected president of the Cambridge Union.

Year	History	Culture
1883	Future Labour PM Clement Attlee born. Britain decides to evacuate the Sudan.	Nietzsche, *Thus Spake Zarathustra*.
1889	Austrian Crown Prince Rudolf commits suicide at Mayerling.	Jerome K Jerome, *Three Men in a Boat*.
1892	Gladstone becomes Prime Minister. Diesel patents his internal combustion engine.	Kipling, *Barrack-Room Ballads*. Tchaikovsky, 'The Nutcracker'.
1897	Russia occupies Port Arthur. Queen Victoria's Diamond Jubilee.	H G Wells, *The Invisible Man*.
1898	Battle of Omdurman. Spanish-American War.	Henry James, *The Turn of the Screw*.
1901	Death of Queen Victoria: succeeded by Edward VII. Boers begin guerrilla warfare in South Africa.	Kipling, *Kim*.
1902	Anglo-Japanese treaty signed. Boer War ends.	Conan Doyle, *The Hound of the Baskervilles*.
1903	Edward VII visits Paris: 'Entente Cordiale' established. Wright Brothers' first flight.	Jack London, *The Call of the Wild*. Film: *The Great Train Robbery*.
1904	Outbreak of Russo-Japanese War.	Chekhov, *The Cherry Orchard*. Puccini, 'Madame Butterfly'.

Year	Age	Life
1905	22	June: Secures a First Class degree (Twelfth Wrangler) in his final undergraduate examinations. Shortly after, begins reading Marshall's *Principles of Economics*, his first foray into economics.
1906	23	October: Starts work as a clerk at the India Office.
1907	24	Becomes bored and frustrated at the India Office. Works on his Fellowship dissertation for King's.
1908	25	March: Fails to secure a King's Fellowship. June: Begins an affair with Duncan Grant. Resigns from the India Office after being offered a lectureship in economics at Cambridge; returns to Cambridge in July.
1909	26	March: First journal article, 'Recent Events in India', appears in the *Economic Journal*. October: Founds the Political Economy Club.
1910	27	Affair with Duncan Grant begins to break down; it ends in 1912.
1911	28	October: Appointed editor of the *Economic Journal*, aged 28.
1913	30	May: Becomes a member of the Royal Commission on Indian Currency and Finance. First book, *Indian Currency and Finance* published by Macmillan
1914	31	Begins speculation activities.

Year	History	Culture
1905	End of Russo-Japanese War: uprisings in Russia. Henry Campbell-Bannerman (Lib.) becomes Prime Minister.	Richard Strauss, 'Salomé'.
1906	Algeciras Conference. US occupies Cuba.	Galsworthy, *The Man of Property*.
1907	Hague Peace Conference. Boy Scout movement founded.	Conrad, *The Secret Agent*.
1908	Lloyd George becomes Chancellor of the Exchequer. Union of South Africa established.	E M Forster, *A Room with a View*.
1909	Blériot crosses the Channel in an aeroplane.	Diaghilev's 'Ballets Russes' appears for the first time in Paris.
1910	Death of Edward VII: succeeded by George V. Dr Crippen executed.	Wells, *The History of Mr Polly*.
1911	Amundsen beats Scott to the South Pole. Lloyd George introduces National Insurance.	Rupert Brooke, *Poems*.
1913	Balkan War.	D H Lawrence, *Sons and Lovers*. Film: the first Charlie Chaplin movies.
1914	Outbreak of the First World War. Battle of Mons; Battle of the Marne; First Battle of Ypres.	James Joyce, *Dubliners*.

Year	Age	Life
1915	32	January: Becomes assistant to Sir George Paish, adviser to Lloyd George. May: Appointed to the Treasury's Finance Division. October: Begins friendship with the Asquiths.
1916	33	January–February: Considers resigning from the Treasury over conscription. Stays in his post, but becomes a conscientious objector. June: Narrowly escapes death after being withdrawn from a party travelling on the ill-fated HMS *Hampshire* carrying Lord Kitchener to Russia. September: Moves into 46 Gordon Square, Bloomsbury.
1917	34	February: Becomes head of the Treasury's 'A' Division. May: Made Companion of the Bath (CB). September: Makes first trip to the US to assist in British efforts to secure loans.
1918	35	March: Interest in collecting art begins with his purchase of Cézanne's *Apples*. October: Meets his future wife, the Russian ballerina Lydia Lopokova.
1919	36	January: The Paris Peace Conference begins; Keynes attends as the Treasury's chief representative. June: Resigns over reparations demands. Begins writing *The Economic Consequences of the Peace*. October: Returns to lecturing at Cambridge. December: *The Economic Consequences of the Peace* published.

Year	History	Culture
1915	First World War: Battles of Neuve Chapelle and Loos. 'Shells scandal'. Gallipoli campaign: death of Rupert Brooke.	John Buchan, *The Thirty-Nine Steps*. Film: *Birth of a Nation*.
1916	First World War: Battle of Verdun; Battle of the Somme. Asquith resigns as PM, replaced by Lloyd George.	James Joyce, *Portrait of an Artist as a Young Man*. Film: *Intolerance*.
1917	First World War: US declares war on Germany; Tsar abdicates in Russia; Battle of Passchendaele. October Revolution in Russia.	P G Wodehouse, *The Man With Two Left Feet*. Film: *Easy Street*.
1918	First World War: Ludendorff's Spring offensive on the Western Front. Allied offensive forces Germany to agree to armistice on 11 November. Murder of Tsar Nicholas II and his family.	Gerald Manley Hopkins, *Poems*. Luigi Pirandello, *Six Characters in Search of an Author*.
1919	Communist Revolt in Berlin. Paris Peace Conference adopts principle of founding League of Nations. Peace Treaty of Versailles signed. US Senate votes against ratification of Versailles Treaty.	Kandinsky, *Dreamy Improvisation*. Film: *The Cabinet of Dr Caligari*.

Year	Age	Life
1920	37	Keynes continues to be consulted on economic policy by the Chancellor. May: Almost goes bankrupt as a result of adverse currency movements.
1921	38	Becomes chairman of the National Mutual Life Assurance Company. August: *A Treatise on Probability* published.
1922	39	January: Replies to critiques of *The Economic Consequences of the Peace* with *A Revision of the Treaty*. April (to January 1923): Writes and edits a series of supplements for the *Manchester Guardian* dealing with 'Reconstruction in Europe'.
1923	40	March: Helps to purchase the Liberal magazine *Nation and Athenaeum*. December: *A Tract on Monetary Reform* published.
1924	41	Appointed First Bursar at King's. November: Starts work on *A Treatise on Money*.
1925	42	July: Publishes *The Economic Consequences of Mr Churchill*. August: Marries Lydia Lopokova. September: Makes the first of three visits to Russia.
1926	43	Breaks with the Asquiths over the General Strike; sides with Lloyd George. March: Purchases Tilton, a farmhouse near Lewes in East Sussex. July: *The End of Laissez-Faire* published.
1927	44	February: Resigns from the University Council at Cambridge.

Year	History	Culture
1920	League of Nations formed. Bolsheviks win Russian Civil War.	F Scott Fitzgerald, *This Side of Paradise.*
1921	Paris Conference fixes Germany's reparation payments. Irish Free State established.	D H Lawrence, *Women in Love.*
1922	Lloyd George's Coalition government falls: Bonar Law becomes PM. British Mandate in Palestine.	Clive Bell, *Since Cezanne.* British Broadcasting Company (later Corporation) (BBC) founded: first radio broadcasts.
1923	French occupy the Ruhr. USSR founded.	P G Wodehouse, *The Inimitable Jeeves.*
1924	Ramsey MacDonald becomes first Labour Prime Minister. Release of 'Zinoviev Letter': Labour loses general election. Baldwin becomes PM.	E M Forster, *A Passage to India.* King George V makes first royal radio broadcast.
1925	Gold Standard in Britain restored by Chancellor of the Exchequer Winston Churchill. Locarno Conference.	Virginia Woolf, *Mrs Dalloway.* Film: *Battleship Potemkin.*
1926	General Strike in the UK. Germany admitted to League of Nations.	Ernest Hemingway, *The Sun Also Rises.*
1927	'Black Friday': collapse of German economy. Trotsky expelled from Communist Party.	Virginia Woolf, *To the Lighthouse.* Film: *The Jazz Singer.*

Year	Age	Life
1929	46	May: Publishes *Can Lloyd George Do It?* with Hubert Henderson. November: Appointed a member of the Macmillan Committee on Finance and Industry and its Economic Advisory Council (EAC).
1930	47	September: Keynes chairs first meeting of the EAC's Committee of Economists. October: *A Treatise on Money* finally appears.
1931	48	January: The 'Circus' starts to meet in Cambridge to discuss *A Treatise on Money*. June: Richard Kahn's article outlining the 'multiplier' principle published in the *Economic Journal*. September: Britain abandons the Gold Standard.
1932	49	Begins work on *The General Theory*.
1933	50	March: *The Means to Prosperity* and *Essays in Biography* are published. June-July: The World Economic Conference in London.
1934	51	May: Has private meeting with President Roosevelt at the White House.
1936	53	3 February: The Cambridge Arts Theatre holds its first performance. 4 February: *The General Theory of Employment, Interest and Money* is published.

Year	History	Culture
1929	Ramsey MacDonald forms second Labour government. The Wall Street Crash.	Virginia Woolf, *A Room of One's Own*.
1930	London Naval Treaty. Crash of the airship *R 101*.	Noel Coward, *Private Lives*. Film: *All Quiet on the Western Front*.
1931	Oswald Mosley splits from Labour Party. MacDonald forms National Government.	Noel Coward, *Cavalcade*. Film: *Dracula*.
1932	Oswald Mosley founds the British Union of Fascists F D Roosevelt elected US President.	Aldous Huxley, *Brave New World*. Film: *Tarzan the Ape Man*.
1933	Hitler appointed Chancellor of Germany. Germany withdraws from League of Nations and Disarmament Conference.	George Orwell, *Down and Out in Paris and London*. Film: *King Kong*.
1934	Anglo-Russian trade agreement. Hitler becomes *Führer* of Germany.	Robert Graves, *I, Claudius*. Film: *David Copperfield*.
1936	Death of King George V. Abdication of Edward VIII; succeeded by George VI. Germany reoccupies the Rhineland. Outbreak of Spanish Civil War.	Penguin Books starts paperback revolution. Film: *Modern Times*. BBC begins world's first television transmission service.

Year	Age	Life
1937	54	May: Suffers heart attack. June–September: Recuperates at Ruthin Castle in North Wales.
1938	55	September: Reads *My Early Beliefs* to the Memoir Club. October: Forced to resign as chairman of the National Mutual Life Assurance Company.
1940	57	February: *How to Pay for the War* published. August: Re-enters the Treasury as an unpaid adviser.
1941	58	May: Travels to America to iron out Britain's Lend-Lease arrangements. September: Becomes a director of the Bank of England.
1942	59	April: Appointed chairman of the Committee for the Encouragement of Music and the Arts (CEMA), forerunner to the Arts Council of Great Britain. June: Becomes Lord Keynes of Tilton.
1943	60	April: The 'White' and 'Keynes' Plans for international monetary stabilisation published. May: Makes maiden speech in the House of Lords.
1944	61	July: Heads the British delegation at Bretton Woods.

Year	History	Culture
1937	Chamberlain succeeds Baldwin as PM. Sino-Japanese War begins.	John Steinbeck, *Of Mice and Men*. Film: *Snow White and the Seven Dwarfs*.
1938	German troops enter Austria. Munich Agreement.	Graham Greene, *Brighton Rock*. Film: *The Adventures of Robin Hood*.
1940	Second World War: German invasion of Norway leads to defeat of Chamberlain: Churchill becomes PM. German invasion of France. The Battle of Britain.	Ernest Hemingway, *For Whom the Bell Tolls*. Film: *The Great Dictator*.
1941	Second World War: Germany invades the USSR. US enters war after Japanese attack on Pearl Harbor	Noel Coward, *Blithe Spirit*. Film: *Citizen Kane*.
1942	Second World War: fall of Singapore; Battle of El Alamein; Battle of Stalingrad; Allied landings in North Africa.	Enid Blyton publishes the first 'Famous Five' book, *Five on a Treasure Island*. Film: *Casablanca*.
1943	Second World War: Axis forces surrender at Stalingrad; Italy surrenders.	Rogers and Hammerstein, *Oklahoma!*
1944	Second World War: D-Day landings in France; assassination attempt on Hitler; Ardennes counter-offensive by Germany.	Terrence Rattigan, *The Winslow Boy*. Film: *Henry V*. Radio: *Much-Binding-in-the-Marsh*.

Year	Age	Life
1945	62	February: Relinquishes editorship of the *Economic Journal*. September–December: Heads a British delegation to the US for loan negotiations.
1946	62	March: Attends the inaugural meeting of the IMF and the World Bank at Savannah, Georgia. 21 April: Dies at Tilton.

Year	History	Culture
1945	Second World War: Roosevelt dies and is succeeded by Truman; Germany surrenders; Japan surrenders after atomic bombs on Hiroshima and Nagasaki.	Evelyn Waugh, *Brideshead Revisited.* Film: *Brief Encounter.*
1946	UN General Assembly opens in London.	Bertrand Russell, *History of Western Philosophy.* Film: *Great Expectations.* Radio: Alistair Cooke's *Letter from America* begins (series ends in 2004).

List of Works

Keynes was a prolific and brilliant writer. His *Collected Works* alone run to 30 volumes. The different channels through which he expressed his views and opinions can be most easily divided into public and private. In the former are Keynes's many books, articles and pamphlets intended for public consumption. Keynes's private thoughts revolve chiefly around his time in government and the many letters he exchanged with friends, family and colleagues. Due to the enormous literature in question, it is impossible to list all of Keynes's publications here. Readers requiring a comprehensive listing should consult *Volume 30: Bibliography and Index* of the *Collected Works*. What follows below is a selection of the more important books and articles published by Keynes during his lifetime.

Abbreviations
EJ = *Economic Journal*
QJE = *Quarterly Journal of Economics*

1909 'Recent Events in India', *EJ* 19 (1909) pp 51–67.
1913 *Indian Currency and Finance.*
1919 December: *The Economic Consequences of the Peace.*
1921 August: *A Treatise on Probability.*
1922 January *A Revision of the Treaty.*
April 1922–January 1923: 'Reconstruction in Europe',

Manchester Guardian.

1923 December: *A Tract on Monetary Reform.*

1924 'Alfred Marshall, 1842–1924', *EJ* 34 (1924) pp 311–72.

1925 July: *The Economic Consequences of Mr Churchill* (Hogarth Press).

August: *Am I a Liberal?*, *Nation and Athenaeum.*

December: *A Short View of Russia* (Hogarth Press).

1926 July: *The End of Laissez-Faire* (Hogarth Press).

1929 May: *Can Lloyd George Do It?* (with Hubert Henderson).

'The Reparation Problem: A Discussion', *EJ* 39 (1929) pp 172–82.

1930 *A Treatise on Money, Volumes 1 and 2.*

October: 'Economic Possibilities for Our Grandchildren', *Nation and Athenaeum.*

1931 *Essays in Persuasion.*

'[Mr. Keynes' Theory of Money]: A Rejoinder', *EJ* 41 (1931) pp 412–13.

'The Pure Theory of Money. A Reply to Dr. Hayek', *Economica* 34 (1931) pp 387–97.

1933 *The Means to Prosperity.*

Essays in Biography.

1936 February: *The General Theory of Employment, Interest and Money.*

1937 'The General Theory of Employment', *QJE* 51 (1937) pp 209–23.

1940 February: *How to Pay for the War.*

1946 'The Balance of Payments of the United States', *EJ* 56 (1946) pp 172–87.

1949 *My Early Beliefs* (posthumous).

Further Reading

Primary Sources

Keynes's *Collected Works* are published in four broad categories to reflect the different aspects of his life. They are: (1) Volumes I–X: books published during Keynes's lifetime; (2) Volumes XI–XIV: professional writings; (3) Volumes XV–XXVII: 'activities'; and (4) Volume XXVIII: social, political and literary writings.

Volume I: Indian Currency and Finance (Macmillan St Martin's Press for the Royal Economic Society: 1971).

Volume II: The Economic Consequences of the Peace (Macmillan St Martin's Press for the Royal Economic Society: 1971).

Volume III: A Revision of the Treaty (Macmillan St Martin's Press for the Royal Economic Society: 1971).

Volume IV: A Tract on Monetary Reform (Macmillan St Martin's Press for the Royal Economic Society: 1971).

Volume V: A Treatise on Money, 1 The Pure Theory of Money (Macmillan St Martin's Press for the Royal Economic Society: 1971).

Volume VI: A Treatise on Money, The Applied Theory of Money (Macmillan St Martin's Press for the Royal Economic Society: 1971).

Volume VII: The General Theory of Employment, Interest and Money (Macmillan Cambridge University Press for the Royal Economic Society: 1973).

Volume VIII: Treatise on Probability (Macmillan for the Royal Economic Society: 1973).

Volume IX: Essays in Persuasion (Macmillan St Martin's Press for the Royal Economic Society: 1972).

Volume X: Essays in Biography (Macmillan St Martin's Press for the Royal Economic Society: 1972).

Volume XI: Economic Articles and Correspondence: Academic, ed. Donald Moggridge (Macmillan Cambridge University Press for the Royal Economic Society: 1983).

Volume XII: Economic Articles and Correspondence: Investment and Editorial, ed. Donald Moggridge (Macmillan Cambridge University Press for the Royal Economic Society: 1983).

Volume XIII: The General Theory and After: Part I, Preparation, ed. Donald Moggridge (Macmillan St Martin's Press for the Royal Economic Society: 1973).

Volume XIV: The General Theory and After: Part II, Defence and Development, ed. Donald Moggridge (Macmillan St Martin's Press for the Royal Economic Society: 1973).

Volume XV: Activities 1906–14: India and Cambridge, ed. Elizabeth Johnson (Macmillan St Martin's Press for the Royal Economic Society: 1971).

Volume XVI: Activities 1914–19: The Treasury and Versailles, ed. Elizabeth Johnson (Macmillan St Martin's Press for the Royal Economic Society, 1971).

Volume XVII: Activities 1920–22: Treaty Revision and Reconstruction, ed. Elizabeth Johnson (Macmillan Cambridge University Press for the Royal Economic Society: 1977).

Volume XVIII: Activities 1922–32: The End of Reparations, ed. Elizabeth Johnson (Macmillan Cambridge University Press for the Royal Economic Society: 1978).

Volume XIX: Activities 1922–29: The Return to Gold and Industrial Policy (in two volumes), ed. Donald Moggridge (Macmillan

Cambridge University Press for the Royal Economic Society: 1981).

Volume XX: Activities 1929–31: Rethinking Employment and Unemployment Policies, ed. Donald Moggridge (Macmillan Cambridge University Press for the Royal Economic Society: 1981).

Volume XXI: Activities 1931–39: World Crises and Policies in Britain and America, ed. Donald Moggridge (Macmillan Cambridge University Press for the Royal Economic Society: 1982).

Volume XXII: Activities 1939–45: Internal War Finance, ed. Donald Moggridge (Macmillan Cambridge University Press for the Royal Economic Society: 1978).

Volume XXIII: Activities 1940–43: External War Finance, ed. Donald Moggridge (Macmillan Cambridge University Press for the Royal Economic Society: 1979).

Volume XXIV: Activities 1944–46: The Transition to Peace, ed. Donald Moggridge (Macmillan Cambridge University Press for the Royal Economic Society: 1979).

Volume XXV: Activities 1940–44: Shaping the Post-War World: The Clearing Union, ed. Donald Moggridge (Macmillan Cambridge University Press for the Royal Economic Society: 1980).

Volume XXVI: Activities 1941–46: Shaping the Post-War World: Bretton Woods and Reparations, ed. Donald Moggridge (Macmillan Cambridge University Press for the Royal Economic Society: 1980).

Volume XXVII: Activities 1940–46: Shaping the Post-War World: Employment and Commodities, ed. Donald Moggridge (Macmillan Cambridge University Press for the Royal Economic Society: 1980).

Volume XXVIII: Social, Political and Literary Writings, ed. Donald Moggridge (Macmillan Cambridge University Press for the Royal Economic Society: 1982).

Volume XXIX: The General Theory and After: A Supplement, ed. Donald Moggridge (Macmillan Cambridge University Press for the Royal Economic Society: 1979).

Volume XXX: Bibliography and Index, ed. Donald Moggridge (Macmillan Cambridge University Press for the Royal Economic Society: 1989).

Secondary Sources

The secondary literature on Keynes is enormous. Any writer (this one included) attempting to present a picture of the many varied aspects of Keynes's life and work owes a huge debt to Lord Robert Skidelsky's magisterial three-volume biography of Keynes. It is easily the most impressive biography of any economist ever written. A one-volume version was published by Macmillan in 2003 under the title, *John Maynard Keynes, 1883–1946: Economist, Philosopher, Statesman*. There are two other full-length treatments of Keynes worthy of mention, that by Harrod published in 1951 (although this glosses over certain aspects of Keynes's life, in particular his sexuality) and, more recently, Donald Moggridge's *Maynard Keynes: An Economist's Biography*, which appeared in 1992. There are also numerous articles, some more technical than others, which the interested reader can refer to. A very small selection appears below:

Asimakopulos, Athanasios, 'Anticipations of Keynes's General Theory?', *Canadian Journal of Economics* 16 (1983) pp 517–30.

Blaug, Mark, 'Second Thoughts on the Keynesian Revolution', *History of Political Economy* 23 (1991) pp 171–92.

Booth, Alan, 'The "Keynesian Revolution" in Economic Policy-making', *Economic History Review* 36 (1983) pp 103–23.

Johnson, Harry G, 'Keynes's General Theory: Revolution or War of Independence?', *Canadian Journal of Economics* 9 (1976) pp 580–94.

Kahn, Richard, 'Some Aspects of the Development of Keynes's Thought', *Journal of Economic Literature* 16 (1978) pp 545–59.

Leijonhufvud, Axel, 'Keynes and the Keynesians: A Suggested Interpretation', *American Economic Review* 57 (1967) pp 401–10.

Patinkin, Don, 'On the Chronology of the General Theory', *Economic Journal* 103 (1993) pp 647–63.

Robinson, Austin, 'John Maynard Keynes 1883–1946', *Economic Journal* 57 (1947) pp 1–68.

Schumpeter, Joseph A, 'John Maynard Keynes 1883–1946', *American Economic Review* 36 (1946) pp 495–518.

Smithies, Arthur, 'Reflections on the Work and Influence of John Maynard Keynes', *Quarterly Journal of Economics* 65 (1951) pp 578–601.

Picture Sources

The author and publishers wish to express their thanks to the following sources of illustrative material and/or permission to reproduce it. They will make the proper acknowledgements in future editions in the event that any omissions have occurred.

Getty Images: pp i, iii, 5, 7, 10, 15, 23, 32, 40, 60, 70, 84, 99, 111. International Monetary Fund: p 119; Topham Picturepoint: pp 47, 127.

Index

29, 61, 67, 76, 80, 83, 94, 102, 114–15
Plesch, Dr Janos, 105

R

Ramsey, Frank, 20, 24
Rankl, Karl, 124
Reading, Lord, 40–1
Reagan, President Ronald, 74, 129
Ricardo, David, 22, 67
Robbins, Lionel, 64, 68–9, 71, 72, 73, 83, 118, 126
Robertson, Dennis, 28, 80, 96, 109, 114, 123
Robinson, Austin, 24, 76, 77, 98
Robinson, Joan, 23, 24, 73, 76, 77–8, 92–3, 101, 102, 114
Roosevelt, President Franklin D, 83–4, 103
Russell, Bertrand, 13

S

Sackville-West, Vita, 33
Samuelson, Paul, 86, 95, 128
Say, Jean-Baptiste, 67
Schumpeter, Joseph, 77
Scott, C P, 56
Shaw, George Bernard, 68, 84, 89
Sheppard, J T, 11

Sidgwick, Henry, 3, 8
Simon, Sir John, 108
Smith, Adam, 22, 67, 104
Sraffa, Piero, 73, 76, 78, 79–80, 104
Stamp, Lord, 114
Stephen, Adrian, 33
Stephen, Sir Leslie, 33
Stephen, Thoby, 33
Stone, Richard, 109–10, 112
Strachey, James, 16
Strachey, Lytton, 12, 13, 16, 17, 33, 34, 46
Strutt, John William, 3
Swithinbank, Bernard, 7

T

Tarshis, Lorie, 103
Tennyson, Alfred Lord, 11
Thatcher, Margaret, 74, 129
Thomson, Logan, 98
Tomlinson, George, 11
Truman, President Harry S, 121
Turing, Alan, 26

V

Vinson, Fred, 124

W

Webb, Beatrice, 68
Webb, Sidney, 68
White, Harry Dexter, 118–22